M000207718

Mysteries of the Soul Expounded

by

Abu Bilal Mustafa al-Kanadi

ISBN 1 898649 53 7

British Library Cataloguing in Publication Data.
A catalogue record for this book is available from the British Library.

Published: Al-Hidaayah Publishing and Distribution

Distributed by: Al-Hidaayah Publishing and Distribution
P.O. Box 3332
Birmingham
United Kingdom
B10 0UH

Tel: 0121 753 1889
Fax: 0121 753 2422
Website: www.al-hidaayah.co.uk
Email: mail@al-hidaayah.co.uk

Mysteries of the Soul Expounded

Contents

Transliteration Table

Consonants,

ء	ʾ	د	d	ض	ḍ	ك	k
ب	b	ذ	dh	ط	ṭ	ل	l
ت	t	ر	r	ظ	ẓ	م	m
ث	th	ز	z	ع	ʿ	ن	n
ج	j	س	s	غ	gh	ه	h
ح	ḥ	ش	sh	ف	f	و	w
خ	kh	ص	ṣ	ق	q	ي	y

Vowels, diphthongs, etc.

Short:	ـَ	a	ـِ	i	ـُ	u
Long:	ـَا	ā	ـِي	ī	ـُو	ū
diphthongs:			ـَيْ	ay	ـَوْ	aw

Foreword

All praise is due to Almighty God, Allāh. We praise Him and seek His help and forgiveness. And we seek refuge in Allāh from the evil of our own selves and from our wicked deeds. Whoever has been guided by Allāh, there is none to misguide him; and whoever has been misguided by Allāh, none can guide him. I bear witness that there is no other god worthy of worship except Allāh, alone, without partner or associate. And I bear witness that Muḥammad is His servant and messenger. May Allāh, the Exalted, bestow His peace and blessings upon Prophet Muḥammad, upon his good and pure family, as well as upon all of the noble companions, and upon those who follow them in righteousness until the Day of Reckoning.

Verily, the most truthful speech is the Book of Allāh, and the best guidance is the guidance of Muḥammad (ﷺ); while the worst affairs are novelties, for every novelty is a (blameworthy) innovation. Every innovation [in matters of religion] is misguidance, and every misguidance is in the Fire.*

The subject of this treatise - the nature, essence and circumstances of the human soul - is fascinating to people of all ages, faiths and walks of life. Personally, I have always been keenly interested in understanding the mysteries of the human soul. After embracing Islām, my desire to know the truth regarding the soul grew even stronger.

In order to fulfill this desire, I read extensively in this area from ancient texts as well as from the works of modern writers

---

* This introductory address constitutes a portion of "*Khuṭbat al-Ḥājah,*" a standard form of opening address used by the Prophet (ﷺ) on certain occasions of import, such as the Friday sermon, the marriage ceremony, etc. A detailed collection of various authentic narrations of this speech can be found in al-Albānī's treatise, *Khuṭbat al-Ḥājah*.

- Islāmic and otherwise. Because of the nature of this exciting topic, one who researches this subject is faced with an enormous amount of conflicting information. Therefore, in order to arrive at sound, dependable conclusions regarding the soul, one must carefully read and analyse the available material and evaluate it according to stringent criteria. This is of utmost importance since it bears directly on one's *ʿaqīdah* (belief and conviction in matters of faith).

During extensive reading and research, I became convinced that Islām, the only fully preserved, divinely revealed faith, had the true answers to man's many questions about the human soul. This conviction compelled me to write a treatise on this most strange and mysterious entity. I hope it will provide beneficial and thought-provoking information for the reader, regardless of his present spiritual inclination.

Throughout this research, I depended upon the glorious Qur'ān since it is the perfectly preserved and unadulterated word of Allāh. Furthermore, I referred to only those prophetic traditions critically assessed to be authentically related and, as such, dependable sources for the subject at hand. Finally, I carefully sifted through the many conflicting views of the scholars who have written in this area and chose only those which are in consonance with the divinely revealed *Sharīʿah* and with sound logic and reasoning.

I trust that what is contained herein will benefit the reader and will have a profound effect on his own thought, faith and way of life. I implore Allāh, the Beneficent and Merciful, to accept this as a work done for His sake alone and to make it a treasure for me on "the Day [of resurrection and judgement) when neither wealth nor sons will benefit [one] except he who comes before Allāh with a sound heart."*

Abū Bilal Muṣṭafā al-Kanadi
Makkah al-Mukarramah
Ramaḍān 1407 A.H./May 1987

---

*True in faith in the one and only Almighty God and sincere in submission to His sacred law. The Qur'ānic quotation is Sūrah *al-Shuʿara'*, 26:88-89.

The Nature and Essence of the Human Soul

Scholars of various schools of thoughts[1] differ greatly regarding the nature and essence of the soul (*nafs*). Is it a part of the physical body or a non-essential characteristic[2] of it? Is it an entity consigned to dwell within the physical body, or is it an independent essence in itself? Is the *nafs* the same as the *rūḥ* (spirit)? Finally, what happens to the soul upon death? Is it confined to its body and its grave? If not, is it free to move about in the unseen spiritual world and on the earth?[3]

Regarding this subject, leading theologians of various sects have put forward a host of conflicting opinions. It would be beyond the scope of the present work to examine each and every view put forward by the various scholars; however, a brief mention of some of their opinions regarding this issue is necessary. The correct

---

[1] Not the four famous schools of *fiqh* (jurisprudence) but rather leading scholars and thinkers who represent various unorthodox sects, such as the Muʿtazilites, Rāfidhites and philosophers. They have expressed various incorrect views and opinions on this and other subjects of *ʿaqīdah*.

[2] In Arabic, *ʿaradh*. According to the terminology of the philosophers, it refers to things which cannot exist independently, like colour, smell, length, etc.

[3] See *Kitāb al-Rūḥ*, p. 272.

view[4] is given, supported by sound reason and statements from the Qur'ān and the authentic sunnah.

Various Incorrect Theories

According to the theologian, Abul-Ḥasan al-Ash'arī, scholars differed regarding the *rūḥ* (spirit), *nafs* (soul) and *ḥayāh* (life force). Al-Nadhdhām, one of the leaders of the Mu'tazilah,[5] is attributed with having said that the *nafs* is the form of the *rūḥ*. He further claimed that the *rūḥ* is alive (i.e., animate) and exists independently. In contrast to his view, other scholars alleged that the *rūḥ* is a non-essential characteristic of the human being, unable to exist independently of itself. Still others opposed both of these views and claimed that it is not known what the *rūḥ* is - an essential characteristic or a non-essential characteristic.

The proponents of another theory claimed that man consists of a particular form contained within a physical body; however, they

---

[4] It is "correct" in the sense that it is not contrary to the beliefs of *ahl al-sunnah*, literally, "the people of the established way or path" (those who sincerely and firmly adhere to the Qur'ān and the authentic sunnah as their complete way of life). Indeed, there is little authentic information about the *ruḥ*. Referring to the *ruḥ* Allāh says in the Qur'ān: وَمَآ أُوتِيتُم مِّنَ ٱلْعِلْمِ إِلَّا قَلِيلًا "And you have not been given knowledge except for a little. " Sūrah *al-Isra'*, 17:85. (ed.)

[5] A misguided sect which introduced speculative dogmatics into Islām. This school of thought is characterised by a slanted, so-called "rationalistic" approach to matters of faith. They interpret clear texts of the *shari'ah* - those from the Qur'ān and the sunnah - in such a manner as to coincide with their preconceived notions based on what they termed "sense." Ibn al-Qayyim has aptly refuted their views and those of others who have been influenced by philosophical thought foreign to Islām. Whoever wishes to delve deeper into this aspect is referred to his celebrated treatise, *Kitāb al-Rūḥ*, pp. 266-293, where he meticulously details his refutation with logic and reasoning.

differed as to precisely what this form is. One group maintained that the form consists of four ingredients[6] from which the physical body originates and further develops. A second opinion was that it represents pure blood, free of impurities and contamination. Another view claimed that this form is the animate life in man, the sensual heat which pervades the body. And a fourth group proposed that the form is an essential element which causes all animate, living beings to function in a particular manner[7] yet is not separated from such beings and does not have a different structure. Although there are other opinions[8] defining this form within the physical body, the four previously mentioned views are a sufficient sample.

The Correct View

What is considered as the most accurate view regarding the *nafs* and the *rūḥ* is that of Ibn al-Qayyim[9] which is affirmed by Ibn Abul-ʿIzz al-Ḥanafi in his commentary on *al-ʿAqīdat al-Ṭaḥāwiyyah*.[10] They base their position on various verses of the Qur'ān and the traditions of the Prophet (ﷺ) as well as on sound logic and rational thought. According to them, man consists of a spirit and a body together. The spirit is an entity which differs from the physical, tangible body. It is a higher type of luminous

---

[6] There is a philosophical view which claims that the human body originates from earth, air, fire and water. However, as mentioned in the Qur'ān and the authentic sunnah, man originates from clay (i.e., earth).

[7] See al-Ghazālī's treatise on the soul, *Maʿārij al-Qudsfee Madārij Maʿārifat al-Nafs*, pp. 27-3 5.

[8] Mentioned and refuted by Ibn Taymiiyyah in *Majmūʿ al-Fatāwā*, vol. 3, pp. 30-35 and vol. 9, pp. 279-302.

[9] See his famous treatise dealing with the circumstances of the soul of the living and the dead, *Kitāb al-Rūḥ*, pp. 249-250.

[10] see pp. 443-444.

(or light-like) being, alive and moving, and it penetrates the limbs, circulating through them as water circulates throughout the petals of a rose, as oil circulates throughout the olive and as fire circulates throughout the burning embers of coal. One may reasonably perceive the soul filling and occupying the body; its form, though nonphysical, is moulded into the body's shape.[11]

The soul will maintain its penetration of the limbs of the physical body and continue to affect their sense, movement and will as long as these limbs remain sound. However, if they are overcome[12] and no longer accept the forces enacted upon them by the soul, the soul leaves the body and enters the spiritual world.

Qur'ānic Evidence

Certain circumstances of the human soul are mentioned in various places of the Qur'ān.[13] Two such examples follow:

ٱللَّهُ يَتَوَفَّى ٱلْأَنفُسَ حِينَ مَوْتِهَا وَٱلَّتِى
لَمْ تَمُتْ فِى مَنَامِهَا ۖ فَيُمْسِكُ ٱلَّتِى قَضَىٰ عَلَيْهَا ٱلْمَوْتَ
وَيُرْسِلُ ٱلْأُخْرَىٰٓ إِلَىٰٓ أَجَلٍ مُّسَمًّى ۚ

"Allāh takes souls at the time of their death [and the souls] of those that do not die during their sleep. He retains those souls

---

[11] Descriptions of the spirit as "light," its mode of penetration of the body, as well as its shape cannot be proven by the Qur'ān or the sunnah. As such, these descriptions can only be considered conclusions based upon their own understanding of the "proofs." (ed.)

[12] Physical accidents, diseases or disorders may destroy the sound, physical harmony and delicate balance of the body's functions, causing a person to die (the point at which the soul leaves the body). In any case, there need not always be a physical dysfunction for divine forces to cause death.

[13] Ibn al-Qayyim identifies over ninety supporting statements from the Qur'ān, the sunnah and sayings of the companions, which altogether give a complete picture of the nature of the human soul and the conditions which surround it. See *Kitāb al-Rūḥ*, pp. 249-261 for details.

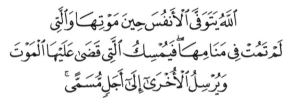

for which He has ordained death, whereas He releases the rest for an appointed term."[14]

In this verse it is stated that there are only two points in time at which Allāh takes souls: at death and during sleep.[15] When one sleeps, Allāh separates the soul from the body. If He has decreed death for a person at this point, the separation becomes permanent and the body no longer functions. In the case of one for whom death has not been decreed at that time, the soul taken during sleep is returned to its respective body upon awakening. However, the soul for which Allāh has decreed death need not necessarily be taken during sleep but may be taken at a time other than sleep.

وَلَوْ تَرَىٰٓ إِذِ ٱلظَّـٰلِمُونَ فِى غَمَرَٰتِ ٱلْمَوْتِ
وَٱلْمَلَـٰٓئِكَةُ بَاسِطُوٓا۟ أَيْدِيهِمْ أَخْرِجُوٓا۟ أَنفُسَكُمُ ٱلْيَوْمَ
تُجْزَوْنَ عَذَابَ ٱلْهُونِ

"If you could see when the wrongdoers taste the pangs of death and the angels stretch their hands out, [saying], 'Deliver up your souls. This day you will be awarded a degrading punishment.'"[16]

Here it is stated that death is painful for the disbelievers. Although they are ordered to surrender their souls to the angels, they are unwilling; therefore, the soul must be forced out as it does not wish to meet its punishment.[17] The terms "*akhrijū anfusakum*" used in this Qur'ānic verse literally mean "expel or push out your souls," indicating that the soul becomes a separate entity from the physical body.

---

[14] Sūrah *al-Zumar*, 39:42.

[15] The separation which occurs during sleep is temporary, whereas, upon death, it is permanent. For details, see al-Rāzī's *al-Tafsīr al-Kabīr*, vol. 26, p. 284.

[16] Sūrah *al-Anʿām*, 6:93.

[17] See al-Qurṭubī's Qur'ānic commentary, *al-Jāmiʿu li Aḥkām al-Qur'ān*, vol. 7, p. 42.

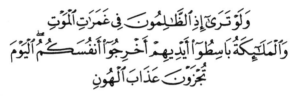

Evidence from the Sunnah

The sunnah is replete with descriptions of the state and nature of the human soul. These hadīths substantiate the view held by the dependable scholars of *ahl al-sunnah*. An example of the physical and psychological punishment awaiting the disbelievers occurs in the following portion of a long, authentically related ḥadīth:

فيقول: أيتها النفس الخبيثة أخرجي إلى سخط من الله وغضب،
قال: فتفرق في جسده فينتزعها كما ينتزع السفود [الكثير
الشعب] من الصوف المبلول، [فتقطع معها العروق والعصب]

> "The Angel of Death [says], 'O you foul soul, come out to the anger and wrath of your Lord,' The soul inside the disbeliever's body is overcome by terrible fear [and does not want to deliver itself up], whereupon the Angel of Death violently pulls it out like multi-pronged skewers being yanked out of wet wool - tearing with them the arteries and nerves."[18]

It is also narrated in an authentic tradition:

دخل رسول الله (ﷺ) على أبي سلمة وقد شق بصره فأغمضه
ثم قال: إن الروح إذا قبض تبعه البصر.

> Umm Salamah reported: "Allāh's Messenger (ﷺ) entered upon Abū Salamah [i.e., his corpse], whose eyes were wide open. The Prophet (ﷺ) closed the lids and then said, 'When the rūḥ (spirit) is taken out, the eyesight follows it [i.e., watches it ascend].'"[19]

These ḥadīths indicate in two ways that the soul is indeed a form. First of all, something must have a form in order to be

---

[18]The full text is related in the section entitled "The Taking of the Soul and the State of the Grave."

[19] Authentically related by Aḥmad and Muslim.

grasped and extracted. And second of all, eyes can only visualize something that has a form.[20]

In another narration the Prophet (ﷺ) described how the believer's soul comes out of the body:

ثم يجيء ملك الموت عليه السلام حتى يجلس عند رأسه فيقول: أيتها النفس الطيبة (وفي رواية: المطمئنة)، أخرجي إلى مغفرة من الله ورضوان، قال: فتخرج تسيل كما تسيل القطرة من في السقاء

"The Angel of Death comes to the [dying] believer, sits at his head and says, 'O you good soul, come out and receive your Lord's forgiveness and pleasure.' Then the soul flows out effortlessly just as water flows from the mouth of a waterskin."[21]

It is related in the same ḥadīth that as the soul is being carried up through the skies, the angels ask, "Who is this?" This question reaffirms the soul's separate existence from the body. The angels would not pose such a question unless they had seen a distinct form.

The following ḥadīth also affirms that the soul separates from the body:

إذا خرجت روح المؤمن تلقاه ملكان فيصعدان إلى السماء، فيقول أهل السماء: روح طيبة جاءت من الأرض، صلى عليك الله، وعلى جسد كنت تعمرينه.

Abū Hurayrah narrated that Allāh's Messenger said.' "When the soul of the believer comes out (of its body), two angels receive it and rise up with it towards the heavens, whereupon

[20] In his *tafsīr*, al-Qurṭubī affirms that the soul has a form. See vol. 15, p. 262.

[21] The full text is related in the section entitled "The Taking of the Soul and the State of the Grave."

> the inhabitants of the heavens say, A good soul has come from the earth. Allāh has blessed you and the body which you used to occupy.'"[22]

The Arabic expression "*kunti ta'murīnah*" ("you used to occupy") suggests that the soul inhabited the body, filling and possessing the whole of it. The soul's dwelling within the body and departure from it clearly confirms the soul's own entity.

[22] Authentically related by Muslim.

The *Nafs* and the *Rūḥ*

An extremely important and highly reasonable question often posed regarding the terms "*nafs*" and "*rūḥ*" is: "Do these terms signify one and the same thing or are they two distinctly different entities?" The majority of Islāmic scholars agree that the *nafs* (soul) and the *rūḥ* (spirit) are two names for one and the same thing. However, others maintain that they are two different entities.[23] The latter is not a tenable position because it lacks clear, unequivocal delineations of these two terms from the texts of the Qur'ān and the sunnah. Rather, it is a result of a misunderstanding of the terminology in these texts and personal conjecture. This is amply illustrated in the following two examples cited in detail by Ibn al-Qayyim.[24]

One group, consisting of some ḥadīth scholars, jurists and Sūfis, states that "the *rūḥ* is other than the *nafs*." Muqātil bin Sulaymān explains this view as follows: "Man has life [*ḥayāh*], a spirit [*rūḥ*] and a soul [*nafs*]. When he sleeps, his *nafs*- with which he senses and understands things -emerges from his body; however, it doesn't completely separate from the physical body. Rather, it extends from it, radiating outward like a cable. While both life and the *rūḥ* remain in his body (being the two means by which he breathes as well as tosses and turns during sleep), man sees visions by means of the *nafs* which emerges from him. When he is about to awaken, his *nafs* returns to him faster than the blinking of an eye.

---

[23] See Ibn al-Ālūsī's *Jalā' al-ʿAynayn*, pp. 142-143 and al-Safārīnī's *Lawāmiʿ al-Anwār*, vol. 2, pp. 31-32.

[24] For a more detailed account of various contradictory opinions, see *Kitāb al-Rūḥ*, pp. 296-297.

However, if Allāh wills that he die in his sleep, He seizes that *nafs* which had come out as described."[25]

Another sector of ḥadīth scholars also holds the opinion that the *rūḥ* is other than the *nafs* but that the *nafs*, which is in the form of man, is dependent upon the *rūḥ* for existence. Man's nature (i.e., *nafs*) is filled with vanities, desires and passions. It is the source of his trials and afflictions, and there is no enemy more hostile to him than his own *nafs*. Thus, the *nafs* wants and loves nothing other than the things of this world, while the *rūḥ* longs for the Hereafter and invites to it.[26]

The two previously stated notions are essentially similar in that they assert that the *nafs* and the *rūḥ* are two separate entities. Other positions exist which are either completely absurd or irrelevant. The absurd views are based on mere personal belief or concepts borrowed from philosophies or teachings foreign to Islām, such as those stating that the *nafs* is earthy and fiery, whereas the *rūḥ* is luminous and spiritual. The irrelevant theories include the conviction that souls are entities whose nature and reality are known only to Allāh, implying that nothing has been revealed to mankind about them.

In contrast, the correct view, as maintained by the vast majority of Muslim theologians and endorsed by the scholars of *ahl al-sunnah*,[27] is that the terms "*nafs*" and "*rūḥ*" are interchangeable. However, the term "*nafs*" is usually applied when the soul is inside the body, and the word "*rūḥ*" is used when the soul is apart from the body.[28] Although these terms may be used interchangeably in

---

[25] Paraphrased from Ibn al-Qayyim's *Kitāb al-Rūḥ*, p. 296.

[26] Ibid .

[27] See *Kitāb al-Rūḥ*, pp. 294-297 and *Jalā' al-ʿAynayn*, pp. 142-143.

[28] This occurs temporarily, during sleep; completely, at death; and throughout the various states encountered thereafter, such as in the grave, in Paradise, etc.

relation to their essence, the difference between them is merely a difference in attributes and usage. Each one has clearly distinct and restricted applications in certain contexts. For example, the term "*nafs*" may be used to mean blood as indicated in saying, "*Salāt nafsuhu.*" ("His blood flowed.") Since death resulting from the flowing of one's blood necessitates the exit of one's soul, blood came to be referred to as "*nafs.*" Additionally; the term "*nafs*" maybe used to mean "the eye" ("*ʿayn*") - commonly referred to as "the evil eye". For instance, it is said, "*Aṣābat fulānan nafsun.*" ("So and so has been struck by an [evil] eye.")[29] Upon occasion, the word "*nafs*" may represent the self (*dhāt*) as evident in a number of Qur'ānic verses such as the following:

فَسَلِّمُوا عَلَىٰٓ أَنفُسِكُمْ
تَحِيَّةً مِّنْ عِندِ ٱللَّهِ مُبَٰرَكَةً طَيِّبَةً

> "Send upon each other [*anfusikum*] a greeting of peace - a greeting from Allāh, blessed and good."[30]

Just as the term "*nafs*" has several different connotations, so does the term "*rūḥ.*" It is never used to refer to the physical body (*badan*) alone or to the soul when it is inside the body. Rather, it has various other usages in the Arabic language and in religious literature.[31] In the following words of Allāh to His Messenger (ﷺ), it is used to mean revelation, specifically, the Qur' an:

وَكَذَٰلِكَ أَوْحَيْنَآ إِلَيْكَ رُوحًا مِّنْ أَمْرِنَا

> "And thus We revealed to you a spirit [i.e., the Qur'ān] by Our command."[32]

---

[29] See Lane's Lexicon, vol. 2, p. 2828.

[30] Sūrah *al-Nūr*, 24:61.

[31] See *al-Ṭaḥāwiyyah*, pp. 444-445 and *Kitāb al-Rūḥ*, pp. 295-296.

[32] Sūrah *al-Shūrā*, 42:52.

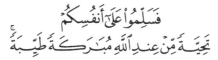

In other places in the Qur'ān the word "*rūḥ*" is used to designate Angel Jibrīl, whom Allāh entrusted with the conveyance of divine revelation. For example:

وَإِنَّهُۥ لَتَنزِيلُ رَبِّ ٱلْعَٰلَمِينَ ﴿١٩٢﴾ نَزَلَ بِهِ ٱلرُّوحُ ٱلْأَمِينُ

"Verily, this [Qur'an] is a revelation of the Lord of the Worlds brought down by the trustworthy spirit [i.e., Jibrīl]."[33]

The various forces and senses contained in the human body are also spoken of as "spirits." Thus it is said, "*al-rūḥ al-bāṣir*" ("the seeing spirit") and "*al-rūḥ al-sāmiʿ*" ("the hearing spirit") and so on. However, these are called "spirits" only by convention. These senses are extinguished upon the death of the physical body, and they are different than the *rūḥ*, which does not die or disintegrate.

Finally, the term "*rūḥ*" is sometimes used in an extremely restricted sense - to designate the spirit of faith which results from one's knowledge of Allāh, from turning to Him in repentance and from seeking Him with love and aspiration. This is the spirit (i.e. consciousness of God) with which Allāh strengthens His obedient, chosen servants as stated in the following Qur'ānic verse:

أُوْلَٰٓئِكَ كَتَبَ فِي قُلُوبِهِمُ
ٱلْإِيمَٰنَ وَأَيَّدَهُم بِرُوحٍ مِّنْهُ

"For those, Allāh has written faith upon their hearts and strengthened them with a spirit from Him."[34]

In this manner, knowledge is a "*rūḥ*" ("spiritual force"), as is sincerity, truthfulness, repentance, love of Allāh and complete dependence upon Him. People differ in respect to these types of spiritual forces. Some are so overcome by them that they become "spiritual" beings. Thus it is said, "So and so has spirit." Others

---

[33] Sūrah *al-Shuʿarā* ; 26:192-193.

[34] Sūrah *al-Mujādilah*, 58:22.

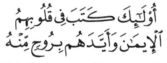

lose the power of such spiritual forces, or the greater portion thereof, and thus become earthly, bestial beings.[35] About them it may be said, "So and so has no spirit; he's empty like a hollow reed," and so on.

Authentic traditions from the Prophet (ﷺ) clearly establish that the *rūḥ* and the *nafs* are essentially one and the same thing. The following narrations, which are two different versions of the same incident, will clarify this point beyond a shadow of a doubt. They explain the manner in which the *rūḥ/nafs* departs from the deceased person's body upon death:

عن أم سلمة أن رسول الله (ﷺ) قال: إن الروح إذا قبض تبعه البصر

> Umm Salamah reported Allāh's Messenger (ﷺ) as saying: "When the *rūḥ* is taken out, the eyesight follows it."

عن أبي هريرة أن رسول الله (ﷺ) قال: ألم تروا الإنسان إذا مات شخص بصره، فذلك حين يتبع بصره نفسه

> Abū Hurayrah reported that the Prophet (ﷺ) said.- "Do you not see that when a person dies his gaze is fixed intently; that occurs when his eyesight follows his nafs [as it comes out]."[36]

Clearly, since the word "*rūḥ*" was used in the first narration and the word "*nafs*" was used in the second, the two terms are, in essence, interchangeable.[37]

---

[35] For more details, see *Lawāmiʿ al-Anwār*, pp. 31-32; *al-Ṭaḥāwiyyah*, p. 445 and *Kitāb al-Rūḥ*, p. 297.

[36] Both of the preceding hadīths are authentic and were related in Muslim's compilation. See also al-Qurṭubī's *al-Tadhkirah*, p. 70.

[37] See also Ṣiddīq Ḥasan Khān's *Fatḥ al-Bayān* vol. 8, p. 232.

The Death Experience

Both the Qur'ān and the traditions of the Prophet (ﷺ) describe death, something all animate creatures must experience. The Qur'ān states:

كُلُّ نَفْسٍ ذَآئِقَةُ ٱلْمَوْتِ

"Every soul will taste death."[38]

Although the term "*nafs*" is used for the soul in this verse, the intended meaning is: "Every creature possessing a soul must die," as will be shown later.

Hardships and Agonies

In the following Qur'ānic verse, Allāh, the Exalted, informs us of the agonies of death.

وَجَآءَتْ سَكْرَةُ ٱلْمَوْتِ بِٱلْحَقِّ ذَٰلِكَ مَا كُنتَ مِنْهُ تَحِيدُ

> "And the agony of death comes, in truth; that is what you wished to avoid."[39]

In this verse the phrase "*sakratul mawt*" (literally, "the drunkenness of death") is used to indicate the swoon of death. This phrase implies that every dying person must experience some pain and torment .[40]

---

[38] Sūrah *Āl ʿImrān*, 3:185.

[39] Sūrah *Qāf*, 50:19.

[40] See al-Alusi's *Rūḥ al-Maʿani*, vol. 26 p. 182 and al-Qurṭubi's *al-Jāmiʿ li Aḥkām al-Qur'ān*, vol. 17, p. 12.

Authentic narrations of the Prophet (ﷺ) also confirm this fact, as related in the following ḥadīth:

عن عائشة أن رسول الله (ﷺ) كانت بين يديه ركوة أو علبة فيها ماء، فجعل يدخل يديه في الماء، فيمسح بهما وجهه ويقول: لا إله إلا الله إن للموت سكرات. ثم نصب يده فجعل يقول: في الرفيق الأعلى. حتى قبض ومالت يده.

ʿĀ'ishah related. "[On the occasion of his approaching death], Allāh's Messenger (ﷺ) had a small vessel of water placed before him. He began to dip his hands in the water, and wiping his face with them, he said, 'There is no one worthy of worship but Allāh! Verily, death brings with it agonies!' Then he raised his hand up and kept repeating, 'In the most exalted company'[41] until his soul was taken and his hand fell limp."[42]

And in another narration:

لقد رأيت رسول الله (ﷺ) وهو بالموت وعنده قدح فيه ماء، وهو يدخل يده في القدح ثم يمسح وجهه بالماء ثم يقول: اللهم أعني على سكرات الموت.

ʿĀ'ishah reported. "Truly, I saw Allāh's Messenger (ﷺ) when death approached him. He had a container with some water in it into which he dipped his hand and then wiped his face. Then he said, 'O Allāh, help me to overcome the agonies of death.'"[43]

---

[41] The Prophet (ﷺ) had been given a choice by Allāh between eternal life and the company of Paradise (i.e., the prophets, their followers, the martyrs and the righteous). The statement quoted was the expression of his choice.

[42] Related by al-Bukhārī.

[43] Related and authenticated by al-Ḥākim.

From what has preceded, it is clear that death causes agony and hardship. Even the Prophet (ﷺ) prayed to Allāh to help him overcome the great test placed upon him. In his treatise on the circumstances of the dead and the Hereafter, al-Qurṭubī emphasized this point. He said, "If such great agonies were experienced upon death by the prophets, the messengers and the pious believers, how can the likes of ourselves be heedless about it - too busy and neglectful in preparing for it? Two benefits can be derived from the occurrence of such agonies and hardships to the chosen prophets (Allāh's blessings be upon them all). The first one is information given to man of the extent of death's pain and calamity. Although one may witness a person's death, one may not observe any fearful movements. Without knowing what the dead person really experienced, one may assume that the person died with ease because it appeared that he expired effortlessly. Thus, man can be sure of the agonies faced by the dying [other than the martyrs] because even though the prophets were especially honoured by Allāh, they still [experienced and] informed us about the fierce pangs of death. The second benefit is the enlightenment of man as to why the beloved of Allāh - the prophets and the messengers - were put through such harsh circumstances. Surely Allāh, the Powerful and Mighty, is capable of alleviating them of all such pain. However, in one of al-Bukhārī's narrations, the Prophet (ﷺ) informed us that the most severely tested are the prophets of Allāh, then the most righteous of other men and then those lesser in degree of righteousness. Thus, even though He could have eased their agonies and lightened the pangs of death, Allāh wished to test them in order to complete their virtues and to raise their degrees [in heaven]. However, it is important to understand that Allāh did not intensify their agony to a point greater than that inflicted upon sinful, disobedient people. The torment that the disobedient must bear is a punishment and a retribution for their sinful conduct. Therefore, there is no comparison between the two."[44]

---

[44] Paraphrased from al-Qurṭubī's *al-Tadhkirah fī Aḥwāl al-Mawtā wa Umūr al-Ākhirah*, p. 22.

The Appearance of Satan

From the preceding, it is obvious that death is a time of great stress, fear and pain for all. There is no doubt that Satan comes even to the dying believer. He is ever present, tempting and troubling one during life, even up to the very point when one's soul exits the body. This continuous harassment is indicated in an authentic ḥadīth:

إن الشيطان يحضر أحدكم عند كل شيء من شأنه حتى يحضره عند طعامه.

> The Prophet (ﷺ) stated: "Verily, Satan comes to you at all circumstances and affairs of your life, even at the time of eating."[45]

It is commonly related that Satan comes to the dying person in the form of certain loved ones, such as his parents, brothers and sisters, friends, etc. and encourages him to die as a Jew or Christian. However, it should be clarified that these "narrations" are not based on authentically related prophetic traditions,[46] but rather, they are stories of people's experiences. Al-Qurṭubī mentions some of these accounts in his *al-Tadhkirah*,[47] stating, "It is said that when

---

[45] Related by Muslim.

[46] Satan's coming in the form of loved ones is mentioned in various Islāmic writings as though it was related from the Prophet (ﷺ) in authentic traditions. For example, see Abū Ḥāmid al-Ghazālī's *Kashf ʿUlūm al-Ākhirah* as mentioned by al-Qurṭubī in his *al-Tadhkirah*, p. 33. It is claimed that al-Tirmidhī and al-Nasāʾī related the following tradition in which the Prophet (ﷺ) is alleged to have said: "Verily, Satan comes to a person at the time of death and says to him, 'Die as a Jew; die as a Christian.'" However, a careful search of these two compilations as well as other ḥadīth literature (such as al-Bukhārī, Muslim, Aḥmad, Abū Dāwūd, Ibn Mājah, al-Dārquṭnī, al-Dārimī, Mālik and others) did not reveal the existence of such a prophetic tradition.

[47] See pp. 33-34.

the time of death approaches the believer, two devils sit near him; one on his right, the other on his left. The one on his right is in the form of his father. He says to the dying person, 'My son, verily I always loved and cared for you; but I died as a Christian, and it is the best of religions.' The devil on his left is in the person of his mother. She says, 'My son, truly my stomach [i.e., womb] was a receptacle for you, my breast a waterskin and my lap a resting place. However, I died as a Jew, and it is the best of religions.'" Al-Qurṭubī continues by stating that Abul-Ḥasan al-Qābisī mentions this description in his commentary on a treatise by Ibn Abī Zayd. Al-Qurṭubī then goes on to explain how the dying person, during the swoon of death and during its agonies, is subjected to various trials and tribulations, as cited previously.

Al-Qurṭubī also mentions that a great number of pious and dependable scholars are known to have witnessed the presence of Satan at death. He relates that he heard one of his own respected teachers, Imām Abul-ʿAbbās Aḥmad bin ʿUmar al-Qurṭubī, say, "I visited the brother of our teacher, Shaykh Abū Jaʿfar Muḥammad al-Qurṭubī, at Cordova and found him near death. It was said to him, 'Repeat: "*Lā ilāha illa Allāh*,"' to which he replied, 'No! No!' When he came round, we mentioned what had occurred. He said, 'Two devils came to me, one on my left and the other on my right. One of them said, "Die as a Jew, for verily it [i.e., Judaism] is the best of religions," while the other said, "Die as a Christian, for truly it [i.e., Christianity] is the best of religions." So I answered them saying, "No! No! How dare you say such a thing to me!"[48]

---

[48] This incident occurred just before the *imām's* death. Since Allāh would never expose one to the unknown realities of death unless one was really going to die, any reports of "near death" experiences (wherein the person recovers and continues to live) are to be treated with skepticism. (ed.)

Repentance Before Death

Surely death is one of the most traumatic experiences which man must undergo. For that reason the Prophet (ﷺ) ordered his followers to seek refuge in Allāh from the *fitnah* (trial and tribulation) of death in the final supplication[49] of every formal prayer:

إذا فرغ أحدكم من التشهد الأخير: فليستعذ بالله من أربع، يقول: اللهم إني أعوذ بك من عذاب جهنم و من عذاب القبر، ومن فتنة المحيا والممات، ومن شر فتنة المسيح الدجال

"When any of you completes the last *tashahhud* of his prayer, let him seek refuge in Allāh from four things, saying, 'O Allāh, verily I seek refuge in You from the punishment of the Hellfire and the torment of the grave; from the *fitnah* of life and of death; and from the evil *fitnah* of the False Messiah.'"[50]

Therefore, every believer should hasten to repent for what sins and shortcomings have preceded, as death may come at any time. Al-Tirmidhī relates the following authentic tradition of the

---

[49] This supplication is made before the closing salutation (*taslīm*) but after the *tashahhud* (which consists of a series of praises to Allāh and a supplication that the peace, mercy and blessings of Allāh be upon Prophet Muḥammad, his family and followers). One may also make additional *duʿā* at this time.

[50] Authentically related by Muslim, al-Nasā'ī and others. The False Messiah (*al-Masīḥ al-Dajjāl*) will appear just before the final hour, and his appearance will be one of the greatest signs signaling its approach. He will claim to be Allāh in person and bear an image of Paradise in one hand and an image of the Hellfire in the other. Those who reject him (i.e., step into his fire) will find themselves in Allāh's Paradise, while those who accept him (i.e., enter his paradise) will find themselves in Allāh's Hellfire. For details, see al-Safārīnī,'s *Lawāmiʿ al-Anwār*, vol. 2, pp. 86-99.

Prophet (ﷺ) indicating the last moment up to which repentance is accepted:

إن الله يقبل توبة العبد ما لم يغرغر

> "Allāh accepts the repentance of the servant so long as his sprit has not arrived at his throat[51] [in its leaving his body upon death]."[52]

Upon the spirit's reaching the throat, the dying person glimpses at what is in store for him - mercy or disgrace; at this point, neither repentance nor the declaration of faith is of any benefit. The Qur'ān states:

فَلَمْ يَكُ يَنفَعُهُمْ إِيمَٰنُهُمْ لَمَّا رَأَوْا۟ بَأْسَنَا

> "Their faith was of no use to them once they saw Our doom."[53]

In another verse there is a clear warning:

وَلَيْسَتِ ٱلتَّوْبَةُ لِلَّذِينَ
يَعْمَلُونَ ٱلسَّيِّـَٔاتِ حَتَّىٰٓ إِذَا حَضَرَ أَحَدَهُمُ ٱلْمَوْتُ
قَالَ إِنِّى تُبْتُ ٱلْـَٰٔنَ

> "Forgiveness is not for those who continue to do evil deeds up until when death comes to one of them [and] be says, 'Truly, I repent now!'"[54]

---

[51] The phrase "so long as his spirit has not arrived at his throat" is literally written in Arabic as "so long as he does not gargle." This expression indicates the gargling noise heard emanating from the dying person's throat as the spirit leaves the body.

[52] Related by, al-Tirmidhī, al-Ḥākim and Ibn Ḥibbān.

[53] Sūrah *Ghāfir*, 40:85.

[54] Sūrah *al-Nisā'*, 4:18.

As illustrated by the preceding examples, the believer must consider the heavy realities of death and prepare for it. It is incumbent upon him to turn to his Lord in repentance lest death seize him unaware, without a chance to seek forgiveness, and lest his lot be one of torment in the grave and/or a term in the Hellfire. As for the disbeliever, he is obliged to hasten to faith in the one and only deity, Almighty God, who is the sole Lord, cherisher and sustainer of all creation - without partner or associate. Furthermore, he must follow the divine guidance revealed to the last chosen prophet and messenger, Muḥammad (ﷺ).

Signs Indicating a Good End

Along with a discussion of the circumstances of death, it is appropriate to highlight those signs which foretell a good end for the deceased believer and consequently, a blissful existence in the life of the Hereafter.

The Pronouncement of the Shahādah

The Prophet (ﷺ) ordered those attending a dying person to prompt him to pronounce the words of the *shahādah* - the testification of *tawḥīd* (unity of Godhood). This has been mentioned in a number of authentic prophetic traditions such as the following:

لقنوا موتاكم لا إله إلا الله. من كان آخر كلامه لا إله إلا الله
دخل الجنة يوما من الدهر، وان أصابه قبل ذلك ما أصابه

"Prompt your dying one to say, '*Lā ilāha illa Allāh*.' He whose last utterance is '*Lā ilāha illa Allāh*,' will enter Paradise- at some time, even if there befalls whatever must befall him before that."[55]

---

[55] Related by Muslim and Ibn Ḥibbān.

The believer who sincerely bears witness to the oneness of Allāh will eventually enter Paradise. However, those who sin and are disobedient to Allāh may have to spend a designated amount of time in the fire of Hell as atonement - assuming that they did not make true repentance or perform the designated act of expiation for their sins. In any case, it is the sole right of Allāh to either punish or extend mercy to them; therefore, every Muslim should hasten to repent and constantly beseech Allāh for forgiveness. Furthermore, one should perform good deeds which please Him, for good works erase evil deeds.

Martyrdom on the Battlefield

True Islāmic *jihād* is a sacred war for the purpose of establishing Allāh's religion on earth and for the defense of the Muslim community and the Islāmic state. The martyr is one who dies in such a war. He is awarded special honour and receives special grace from Allāh's bounty - a befitting reward for one who sacrifices his life solely for Allāh's cause. It is written in the Qur' an:

وَلَا تَحْسَبَنَّ ٱلَّذِينَ قُتِلُوا۟ فِى
سَبِيلِ ٱللَّهِ أَمْوَٰتًۢا ۚ بَلْ أَحْيَآءٌ عِندَ رَبِّهِمْ يُرْزَقُونَ ﴿١٦٩﴾ فَرِحِينَ
بِمَآ ءَاتَىٰهُمُ ٱللَّهُ مِن فَضْلِهِۦ وَيَسْتَبْشِرُونَ بِٱلَّذِينَ لَمْ يَلْحَقُوا۟
بِهِم مِّنْ خَلْفِهِمْ أَلَّا خَوْفٌ عَلَيْهِمْ وَلَا هُمْ يَحْزَنُونَ ﴿١٧٠﴾
۞ يَسْتَبْشِرُونَ بِنِعْمَةٍ مِّنَ ٱللَّهِ وَفَضْلٍ وَأَنَّ ٱللَّهَ لَا يُضِيعُ أَجْرَ
ٱلْمُؤْمِنِينَ ﴿١٧١﴾

> "Do not consider those who are slain in the path of Allāh as dead. Rather, they are alive with their Lord, being provided for. They are happy with what Allāh has bestowed upon them of His bounty. And they rejoice in the glad tidings given to those [of their brethren] who have been left behind and have not yet joined them -that no fear shall overcome them, nor

shall they grieve. They rejoice in Allāh's grace and bounty and in the fact that Allāh does not allow the reward of believers to be lost."[56]

Allāh specifically directs us not to consider those slain in *jihād* dead; for, in reality, they are alive with a life much more beautiful, joyful and noble than earthly life. Their spirits have been freed to roam about in the gardens of Paradise and to delight in some of its pleasures. In an authentic tradition the Prophet (ﷺ) described some of the special graces conferred upon martyrs:

للشهيد عند الله ست خصال: يغفر له في أول دفعة من دمه، ويرى مقعده من الجنة، ويجار من عذاب القبر، ويأمن الفزع الأكبر، ويحلى حلية الإيمان، ويزوج من الحور العين، ويشفع في سبعين إنسان من اقاربه

"Allāh has prepared for the martyr six[57] special distinctions: he will be forgiven upon the first outpouring of his blood; he will see his place in Paradise; he will be protected from the torment of the grave and from the horrors of *al-Faz' al-Akbar* [The Great Terror][58] and he will be decorated with the adornment of faith, wedded to the women of Paradise and will be allowed to intercede on behalf of seventy relatives."[59]

---

[56] Sūrah *Āl 'Imrān*, 3:169-171.

[57] It actually appears that there are seven mentioned, but the torment of the grave and the horrors of *al-Faz' al-Akbar* are counted as one, thus making it six. Furthermore, those mentioned are not the only aspects of distinction, as others have been related in the Qur'ān and authentic sunnah.

[58] This refers to the horrors of the Resurrection - the fear which will grip the disbelievers, hypocrites and wrongdoers at the time of Judgement when there will be questioning, accounting and ordering of some to the Fire. For details, see 'Allāmah Ṣiddīq Ḥasan Khān's *Fatḥ al-Bayān fī Maqāṣid al-Qur'ān* vol. 6, p. 192.

[59] Authentically related by al-Tirmidhī, Aḥmad, et. al.

Death in the Path of Allāh

If the *mujāhid* (warrior) is not actually killed on the battlefield but dies due to natural causes or an accident while in Allāh's path, he is still considered a martyr and will enjoy the favour and blessings of Allāh. This was clearly pointed out by Allāh's Messenger (ﷺ) in the following ḥadīth:

من فصل في سبيل الله فمات أو قتل فهو شهيد، أو وقصه فرسه أو بعيره، أو لدغته هامة، أو مات على فراشه بأي حتف شاء الله، فإنه شهيد، وإن له الجنة

"Whoever goes out in Allāh's path and then dies or is slain is a martyr; so, too, is one a martyr if he dies from being thrown by his horse or camel [during jihād], or [from being] bitten by a venomous creature[60] [during jihād], or even [if he] dies on his bed for any [other] reason willed by Allāh [during *jihād*]. Such is a martyr, and for him there is Paradise."[61]

Similarly, the warrior who is stationed in readiness for *jihād* is considered a martyr if he dies while in a state of preparedness. The Prophet (ﷺ) said regarding such a person:

كل ميت يختم على عمله إلا الذي مات مرابطا في سبيل الله، فإنه ينمى له عمله إلى يوم القيامة، ويأمن فتنة القبر، و في رواية للطبراني زاد: ويبعث يوم القيامة شهيدا

"Every deceased person's works are sealed [by his death][62] except for the warrior at his station who died in the path of

---

[60] If he is stung or bitten by a poisonous snake, lizard, insect, scorpion, etc., ultimately leading to his death.

[61] Authentically related by Abū Dāwūd, al-Bayhaqī and al-Ḥākim.

[62] He can no longer perform deeds which will be to his benefit. However, it is clear from certain texts from the Qur'ān and the sunnah that parents benefit from the works of their pious children, and a person benefits continuously from what he has left behind by way of useful projects, writings and continuous charity which increase his rewards in the Hereafter.

Allāh; for indeed his deeds are increased until the Day of Resurrection, and he is protected from the trial of the grave. [Additionally, in a narration from al-Ṭabarānī, the Prophet (ﷺ) said], And he will be raised up as a martyr on the Day of Resurrection."[63]

Death Due to Diseases or Accidents

Death which is caused by certain diseases or accidents as specified in the sunnah also bears tidings of a good end. The following tradition concerns the plague, in particular:

عن عائشة أنها سألت رسول الله (ﷺ) عن الطاعون. فأخبرها نبي الله (ﷺ): إنه كان عذابا يبعثه الله على من يشاء، فجعله الله رحمة للمؤمنين، فليس من عبد يقع في الطاعون، فيمكث في بلده صابرا يعلم أنه لن يصيبه إلا ما كتب الله له، الا كان له مثل أجر الشهيد

'Ā'ishah related that she asked the Messenger of Allāh (ﷺ) about the plague, and he informed her. "It is a form of punishment which Allāh sends upon whom He pleases. However, Allāh has made it [a form of] mercy for believers. If when the plague occurs a believing servant stays in his land patiently in the knowledge that nothing can happen to him other than what Allāh has decreed for him, then he will have a reward like that of a martyr."[64]

In addition to this, other diseases and accidents are mentioned in the following tradition of the Prophet (ﷺ):

---

[63] Related by al-Tirmidhī, Aḥmad and others with a dependable chain of transmitters.

[64] Authentically related by al-Bukhārī, Aḥmad, et. al.

الشهداء سبعة سوى القتل في سبيل الله: المطعون شهيد، والغريق شهيد، وصاحب ذات الجنب شهيد، والمبطون شهيد، والحريق شهيد، والذي يموت تحت الهدم شهيد، والمرأة تموت بجمع شهيدة، وفي رواية من أحمد: والسل شهادة

"Martyrs other than those slain in the path of Allāh are seven: the one overcome by plague, the drowned person, the one who dies of pleurisy,[65] the one who succumbs to stomach disease,[66] the one who dies in a fire or under a collapsed object, [67] and the woman who dies during her pregnancy or delivery."[68] [And in a narration from Aḥmad: "Death from consumption[69] is martyrdom."]

Death in Defence of One's Rights

Those who die defending themselves, their family, their wealth, their faith or any other legal right or who are wrongfully killed by those who practice injustice and tyranny are considered to have the reward of martyrs. The following traditions bear witness to this fact:

من قتل دون ماله فهو شهيد، ومن قتل دون أهله فهو شهيد، ومن قتل دون دينه فهو شهيد، ومن قتل دون دمه فهو شهيد

[65] A medical condition which is characterized by inflammation of the pleura, a delicate serous membrane lining each half of the breast plate and folded back over the surface of the lung of the same side. It is accompanied by fever, difficult and painful respiration, and coughing.

[66] Such as dysentery, poisoning, etc.

[67] Such as a wall, a house or a landslide.

[68] Related by Mālik, Abū Dāwūd, et. al. with a dependable chain of transmitters.

[69] Characterized by slow deterioration of the body.

The Prophet (ﷺ) said. "Whoever is killed defending his wealth or possessions is a martyr; whoever dies defending his family is a martyr; whoever is slain because of his faith[70] is a martyr; and whoever dies defending himself is a martyr."[71]

من قتل دون مظلمته فهو شهيد

Allāh's Messenger (ﷺ) said: "Whoever is killed as a result of tyranny and injustice[72] is a martyr."[73]

Death on Jumuʿah (Friday)

There is a special grace and mercy from Allāh, the Blessed and Exalted, for those believing Muslims whose lives He takes on *Jumuʿah*, the day of congregational prayer. It is reported that Allāh's Messenger (ﷺ) said:

ما من مسلم يموت يوم الجمعة، أو ليلة الجمعة، إلا وقاه الله فتنة القبر

"There is no Muslim who dies on *Jumuʿah* [Friday] or on the eve before it[74] that is not protected by Allāh from the trials and torment of the grave."[75]

---

[70] Simply because he believes in Islām, is active in inviting to it, etc.

[71] Compiled by Abū Dāwūd, al-Nasā'ī and others with an authentic chain of transmitters.

[72] Such as being tortured to death in prison at the order of a tyrannical ruler, being assassinated, etc.

[73] Compiled by al-Nasā'ī with a dependable chain of transmitters.

[74] According to Islāmic definition, the day begins at sunset and continues until the following sunset. Thus *laylat al-Jumuʿah* (Friday evening) begins at sunset on Thursday.

[75] Related by Aḥmad, al-Tirmidhī, et. al. with a dependable chain of transmitters.

The Perspiring Brow upon Death

A perspiring brow at the time of death is also a sign bearing good tidings for a Muslim:

عن بريدة بن الخصيب أنه كان بخراسان، فعاد أخا له وهو مريض، فوجده بالموت، وإذا هو بعرق جبينه، فقال: الله أكبر! سمعت رسول الله (ﷺ) يقول: موت المؤمن بعرق جبينه

Buraydah bin al-Khaṣib related that he was in Khurāsān where he visited a brother who was ill and found him dying, his brow covered with perspiration. Thereupon he cried. "*Allāhu Akbar*! Verily, I heard Allāh's Messenger (ﷺ) say, 'The death of a believer is [accompanied by] perspiration on the brow.'"[76]

Death During or After Good Deeds

It is considered a good sign when death occurs during one's engagement in acts of piety and worship or shortly thereafter. A number of dependable narrations traced to the Prophet (ﷺ) attest to this:

من قال لا إله إلا الله ابتغاء وجه الله ختم له بها دخل الجنة، و من صام يوما ابتغاء وجه الله ختم له بها دخل الجنة، ومن تصدق بصدقة ابتغاء وجه الله ختم له بها دخل الجنة

"Whoever (sincerely) pronounced the *shahādah* [i. e., *lā ilāha illa Allāh*] seeking the pleasure of Allāh as his last act will enter Paradise .[77] Whoever fasted a day, seeking Allāh's

[76] Collected by Aḥmad and al-Nasā'ī with an authentic chain of transmitters.

[77] This is to be taken as a good omen regarding his final state of affairs. However, it does not mean that he does not have to expiate for certain sins - especially those committed against fellow man and society - as these can only be settled on the Day of Accounts. His sins against and disobedience to Allāh are left to Allāh's mercy and justice.

pleasure - and it was his last act- will enter Paradise. And whoever gave charity, seeking Allāh's pleasure - and it was his last deed - will enter Paradise."[78]

May Allāh, the Almighty, in His beneficence and mercy, grant us His favour and grace so that our souls are taken while we are in the most pleasing state; and may He protect us from the torment of the grave and the fire of *Jahannam*.[79] May Allāh, in His infinite mercy, admit us into His Paradise without any settling of accounts or reckoning. Truly, He is the Compassionate, the Forgiving, the Merciful.

---

[78] Authentically related by Aḥmad.

[79] One of the various names for the Hellfire.

The Taking of the Soul and the State of the Grave

There are a number of authentic traditions detailing how the souls of the believers and disbelievers are taken out of the bodies, brought towards Heaven and finally, back to their respective bodies and graves. Furthermore, there are detailed descriptions of the circumstances of the body and soul in the grave and in the *barzakh*.[80] The traditions which report the manner and circumstances in which the soul is extracted, taken up, etc. vary slightly in length and wording. The following synthesis[81] of relevant hadīths is quoted in order to create an all-encompassing picture:

عن البراء بن عازب قال: خرجنا مع النبي (ﷺ) في جنازة رجل من الأنصار، فانتهينا إلى القبر ولما يلحد، فجلس رسول الله (ﷺ) [مستقبل القبلة]، وجلسنا حوله، وكأن على رؤوسنا الطير، وفي يده عود ينكت في الأرض، [فجعل ينظر إلى السماء، وينظر إلى الأرض، وجعل يرفع بصره ويخفضه، ثلاث]، فقال: استعيذوا بالله من

---

[80] Literally, "a barrier between two things." Here it indicates a state between the physical worldly existence and the life after the Resurrection and Judgement. See Abū Bakr al-Jazā'irī's *'Aqīdat al-Mu'min*, p. 393 and 'Abdur-Raḥmān al-Maydānī's *al-'Aqīdat al-Islāmiyyah wa Ususuhā*, p. 643.

[81] By Muḥammad Nāṣiruddīn al-Albani. It contains authentic narrations from the compilations of Abū Dāwūd, Ibn Mājah, al-Ḥākim, al-Nasā'ī and al-Ṭayālisī. See *Aḥkām al-Janā'iz*, pp. 156-159.

عذاب القبر، مرتين، أو ثلاثا، [ثم قال، اللهم إني أعوذ بك من عذاب القبر][ثلاث]، ثم قال: إن العبد المؤمن إذا كان في انقطاع من الدنيا، وإقبال من الآخرة، نزل إليه ملائكة من السماء، بيض الوجوه، كأن وجوههم الشمس، معهم كفن من أكفان الجنة، وحنوط من حنوط الجنة، حتى يجلسوا منه مد البصر، ثم يجيء ملك الموت عليه السلام حتى يجلس عند رأسه فيقول: أيتها النفس الطيبة (وفي رواية: المطمئنة)، أخرجي إلى مغفرة من الله ورضوان، قال: فتخرج تسيل كما تسيل القطرة من في السقاء، فيأخذها، (وفي رواية: حتى إذا خرجت روحه صلى عليه كل ملك بين السماء والأرض، و كل ملك في السماء، و فتحت له أبواب السماء، ليس من أهل باب إلا وهم يدعون الله أن يعرج بروحه من قبلهم)، فإذا أخذها لم يدعوها في يده طرفة عين حتى يأخذوها فيجعلوها في ذلك الكفن، وفي ذلك الحنوط، فذلك قوله تعالى:﴿تَوَفَّتْهُ رُسُلُنَا وَهُمْ لاَ يُفَرِّطُونَ﴾، ويخرج منها كأطيب نفحة مسك وجدت على وجه الأرض، قال: فيصعدون بها فلا يمرون -يعني- بها على ملأ من الملائكة إلا قالوا: ما هذا الروح الطيب؟ فيقولون: فلان ابن فلان بأحسن أسمائه التي كانوا يسمونه بها في الدنيا، حتى ينتهوا بها إلى السماء الدنيا، فيستفتحون له، فيفتح لهم، فيشيعه من كل سماء مقربوها، إلى السماء التي تليها، حتى ينتهي به إلى السماء السابعة، فيقول الله عز وجل: اكتبوا كتاب عبدي في عليين، [﴿وَمَا أَدْرَاكَ مَا عِلِّيُّونَ. كِتَابٌ مَّرْقُومٌ يَشْهَدُهُ الْمُقَرَّبُونَ﴾] فيكتب كتابه في عليين، ثم يقال]، أعيدوه إلى الأرض، فإني [وعدتهم أني] منها خلقتهم، وفيها أعيدهم ومنها أخرجهم تارة أخرى، قال: [فيرد إلى الأرض، و] تعاد روحه في جسده، [قال، فإنه يسمع خفق

نعال أصحابه إذا ولوا عنه] [مدبرين]، فيأتيه ملكان [شديدا الانتهار][فينتهرانه]، ويجلسانه فيقولان له: من ربك؟ فيقول: ربي الله، فيقولان له: ما دينك؟ فيقول: ديني الإسلام، فيقولان له: ما هذا الرجل الذي بعث فيكم؟ فيقول: هو رسول الله (ﷺ)، فيقولان له: وما عملك؟ فيقول: قرأت كتاب الله، فآمنت به، وصدقت، [فينتهره فيقول: من ربك؟ ما دينك؟ من نبيك؟ وهى آخر فتنة تعرض على المؤمن، فذلك حين يقول الله عز وجل: ﴿يُثَبِّتُ اللّهُ الَّذِينَ آمَنُواْ بِالْقَوْلِ الثَّابِتِ فِي الْحَيَاةِ الدُّنْيَا﴾ فيقول: ربي الله، وديني الإسلام، ونبيي محمد (ﷺ)]، فينادي مناد في السماء: أن صدق عبدي، فافرشوه من الجنة، وألبسوه من الجنة، وافتحوا له بابا إلى الجنة، قال: فيأتيه من ريحها وطيبها، ويفسح له في قبره مد بصره، قال: ويأتيه [وفي روايه: يمثل له] رجل حسن الوجه، حسن الثياب، طيب الريح، فيقول: أبشر بالذي يسرك، [أبشر برضوان من الله، وجنات فيها نعيم مقيم]، هذا يومك الذي كنت توعد، فيقول له: [وأنت فبشرك الله بخير] من أنت؟ فوجهك الوجه يجيء بلخير، فيقول: أنا عملك الصالح [فوالله ما علمتك إلا كنت سريعاً في طاعة الله، بطيئاً في معصية الله، فجزاك الله خيراً]، ثم يفتح له باب من الجنة، وباب من النار، فيقال: هذا منزلك لو عصيت الله، أبدلك الله به هذا فإذا رأى ما في الجنة قال: رب عجل قيام الساعة، كيما أرجع إلى أهلي ومالي، [فيقال له: اسكن] قال: وإن العبد الكافر (وفي رواية: الفاجر) إذا كان في انقطاع من الدنيا، وإقبال من الآخرة، نزل إليه من السماء ملائكة [غلاظ شداد]، سود الوجوه، معهم المسوح [من النار]، فيجلسون منه مد البصر، ثم يجيء ملك الموت حتى يجلس عند رأسه، فيقول: أيتها النفس الخبيثة أخرجي

إلى سخط من الله وغضب، قال: فتفرق في جسده فينتزعها كما ينتزع السفود [الكثير الشعب] من الصوف المبلول، [فتقطع معها العروق والعصب]، [فيلعنه كل ملك بين السماء والأرض، وكل ملك في السماء، وتغلق أبواب السماء، ليس من أهل باب إلا وهم يدعون الله ألا تعرج روحه من قبلهم]، فيأخذها، فإذا أخذها، لم يدعوها في يده طرفة عين حتى يجعلوها في تلك المسوح، ويخرج منها كأنتن ريح جيفة وجدت على وجه الأرض، فيصعدون بها، فلا يمرون بها على ملأ من الملائكة إلا قالوا: ما هذا الروح الخبيث؟ فيقولون: فلان ابن فلان بأقبح أسمائه التي كان يسمى بها في الدنيا، حتى ينتهي به إلى السماء الدنياء، فيستفتح له: فلا يفتح له، ثم قرأ رسول الله (ﷺ): ﴿لاَ تُفَتَّحُ لَهُمْ أَبْوَابُ السَّمَاء وَلاَ يَدْخُلُونَ الْجَنَّةَ حَتَّى يَلِجَ الْجَمَلُ فِي سَمِّ الْخِيَاطِ﴾ فيقول الله عز وجل: اكتبوا كتابه في سجين، في الأرض السفلى، [ثم يقال: أعيدوا عبدي إلى الأرض فإني وعدتهم أني منها خلقتهم، وفيها أعيدهم، ومنها أخرجهم تارة أخرى]، فتطرح روحه [من السماء] طرحا [حتى تقع في جسده] ثم قرأ ﴿وَمَن يُشْرِكْ بِاللَّهِ فَكَأَنَّمَا خَرَّ مِنَ السَّمَاءِ فَتَخْطَفُهُ الطَّيْرُ أَوْ تَهْوِي بِهِ الرِّيحُ فِي مَكَانٍ سَحِيقٍ﴾ فتعاد روحه في جسده، [قال فإنه ليسمع خفق نعال أصحابه إذا ولوا عنه]. ويأتيه ملكان [شديدا الانتهار، فينتهرانه]، ويجلسانه، فيقولان له: من ربك؟ [فيقول: هاه هاه، لا أدري، فيقولان له: ما دينك؟ فيقول: هاه هاه، لا أدري] فيقولان: فما تقول في هذا الرجل الذي بعث فيكم؟ فلا يهتدي لإسمه، فيقال: محمد! فيقول: هاه هاه، لا أدري [سمعت الناس يقولون ذلك! قال: فيقال: لا دريت]، [ولا تلوت]، فينادي مناد من السماء أن كذب،

فافرشوا له من النار، وافتحوا له بابا إلى النار، فيأتيه من حرها وسمومها، ويضيق عليه قبره حتى تختلف فيه أضلاعه، ويأتيه (وفي رواية: ويمثل له) رجل قبيح الوجه، قبيح الثياب، منتن الريح، فيقول: أبشر بالذي يسوؤك، هذا يومك الذي كنت توعد، فيقول [وأنت فبشرك الله بالشر] من أنت؟ فوجهك الوجه يجيء بالشر! فيقول: أنا عملك الخبيث، [فوالله ما علمتك إلا كنت بطيئا عن طاعة الله، سريعا إلى معصية الله]، [فجزاك الله شرا، ثم يقيض له أعمى أصم أبكم في يده مرزبة! لو ضرب بها جبل كان ترابا، فيضربه ضربة حتى يصير بها ترابا، ثم يعيده الله كما كان، فيضربه ضربة أخرى، فيصيح صيحة يسمعه كل شيء إلا الثقلين، ثم يفتح له باب من النار، ويمهد من فرش النار]، فيقول: رب لا تقم الساعة.

It is reported that al-Barā' bin ʿĀzib said.. "We went out with the Prophet (ﷺ) in order to participate in the funeral rites of a man from the Anṣār.[82] We arrived at the grave, but the inner chamber had not been prepared yet; so Allāh's Messenger (ﷺ) sat down facing the direction of the qiblah,[83] and we sat around him so attentively that it was as if birds were sitting upon our heads.[84] He had a stick in his hand with which he sketched upon the ground. Then he began looking alternately to the heavens and to the earth, raising his gaze and then lowering it. Finally, he said two or three times, 'Seek

---

[82] The name given to the people of Madīnah who believed in the Prophet's message and gave him full assistance in his emigration to their land. They pledged their support for his cause and helped him to establish the new Islāmic state. Thus, they were called al-Anṣār (literally, "the helpers").

[83] The direction which Muslims face during prayer - towards the Kaʿbah (the first house of worship built by Prophet Abraham) in Makkah.

[84] An Arabic expression indicating the intensity of their attentiveness.

refuge in Allāh from the torment of the grave.' Then he said, 'O Allāh, verily I seek refuge in You from the torment of the grave.' He repeated it three times, then he elaborated, 'Verily, when the believing servant is leaving this world and entering the next, angels[85] from the heavens descend to him -their faces white with brightness like the sun and carrying with them burial sheets and scents[86] from Paradise. They sit before him at a distance as far as the eye can see. Then the Angel of Death (upon whom be peace) comes to the person, sits at his head and says, "O good soul [and in another narration "O confident soul"], come out to your Lord's forgiveness and pleasure."' [The Prophet (ﷺ) continued], 'Thereupon, the soul flows out of the body like water flowing from the mouth of a waterskin, and all of the angels between the skies and the earth supplicate for Allāh's blessing upon him. The doors of the heavens are opened for him, and the keepers of these doors [i. e., the angels] all plead with Allāh that this soul might pass in front of them as it is being carried upward. The Angel of Death barely receives the soul in his hands, whereupon the other angels take it from him and wrap it with fragrant winding sheets. This is what is meant by Allāh's saying, "Our messengers [i.e., angels] seize his soul, and they do not fall short of their duty."'[87] Then the Prophet (ﷺ) said, 'There exudes from the soul a scent like the most beautiful fragrance of musk that one could find on the face of the earth. The angels ascend with the soul, never passing a host of angels without hearing them ask, "Who is this wonderful soul?" They reply, "So and so, the son of so and so," addressing him with the best names he was known by during his earthly life. Upon reaching the first heaven, the angels request that it be opened for the soul - which is granted. The soul is then

---

[85] As recorded in some authentic narrations related by Aḥmad and others, these are the "angels of mercy."

[86] Called *ḥanūṭ*, anything by which a corpse is perfumed in preparation for burial.

[87] Sūrah *al-Anʿām*, 6:61.

accompanied by the angels of each heaven until it reaches the one above it and finally arrives at the seventh heaven. Then Allāh, the Mighty and Majestic, says [to the angels], "Place the record of My servant in *ʿilliyyūn*.'"[88] The person's record is then placed in ʿilliyyūn, whereupon a command is heard: "Return him to the earth, for verily I have promised mankind that having created them from the earth, I will return them to it. And I will make them come out of it, yet another time."[89] Then the soul is retumed to the earth, back into its body. Verily, the deceased hears the shuffling feet of his companions who attended his burial as they turn away and leave his grave. Thereupon, two angels,[90] severe in interrogation, come to him, and sitting him up, they begin to ask him questions. They say, "Who is your Lord?" He replies, "Allāh is my Lord." They continue, "What is your religion?" He answers, "Islām is my religion." They proceed with the questioning, saying, "Who is this man that has been sent to you?" He

---

[88] "And what will explain to you what '*ʿilliyyun*' is? [It is] a written record, witnessed by those brought near to their Lord." Sūrah *al-Muṭaffifīn*, 83:19-21. Commentators differ as to the meaning of the term "*ʿilliyyun*." These verses refer to it as a written book or record. It is said that this book records all of the good deeds of the angels, of the believers from among mankind and of the believers from among the *jinn*. Its being "witnessed by those brought near to their Lord" refers to the angels who attend to it and guard it. For details, see al-Ālūsī's *Rūḥ al-Maʿānī*, vol. 30, p. 74.

[89] The time just before the Judgement, when the horn is blown and when the souls come out of the graves and come before Allāh. See Sūrah *Ṭā Hā*, 20:55.

[90] In an authentic , ḥadīth related by al-Tirmidhī the Prophet (ﷺ) described them as bluish-black. One of them is named Munkar, and the other is called Nakīr. See *al-ʿAqīdat al-Ṭaḥāwiyyah*, p. 450. A more complete description of them is in a narration related by Aḥmad and authenticated by al-Mundhirī in his *al-Targhīb wat-Tarhīb*, vol. 4, p. 369. They are described as having voices which rumble like thunder and eyes which flash like lightning, and they have fangs which are capable of tearing the earth asunder.

responds, "He is the Messenger of Allāh (ﷺ)." Finally, they ask him about his deeds, to which he replies, "I read Allāh's Book and believed in it."' (In another narration the Prophet (ﷺ) indicated that the angels ask, "Who is your Lord, what is your religion and who is your prophet?" [Allāh's Messenger (ﷺ) explained that] this was the believer's last test, and it is what is meant when Allāh says, "Allāh strengthens those who believe with a firm testimony in this worldly life and in the Hereafter."[91] The deceased answers, "Allāh is my Lord, Islām is my religion, and my prophet is Muḥammad.") [The Prophet (ﷺ) then indicated, 'Upon the believer's answer to these questions], a voice is heard in the heavens, saying, "My servant has told the truth, so clothe him in the clothing of Paradise, spread for him the furnishings of Paradise, and open for him a window with a view of Paradise." Thereupon, he is engulfed by a breeze of fresh air and fragrance, while the expanse of his grave is extended before him as far as the eye can see. There appears before him a man with a wonderful face and beautiful clothing, emitting a splendid fragrance. He says to the soul, "Rejoice at the news which will gladden you! Rejoice at Allāh's pleasure and His Paradise, whose joys and delights never end. This is the day which you were promised." The deceased says to him, "And who are you, for your face bears glad tidings?!" The figure answers, "I represent your good deeds; by Allāh, I've always known you to be quick in obedience to Allāh and slow to His disobedience. So may Allāh award you with good." Then a door to Paradise is opened, and a door to the Fire is opened, whereupon it is said to him [regarding the Hellfire], "This would have been your final abode had you disobeyed Allāh;[92] however, it has been

---

[91] Sūrah *Ibrāhīm*, 14:27.

[92] Such disobedience includes rejecting Allāh's invitation to accept Him as the sole Lord, Cherisher and Sustainer and the sole God worthy of worship. Allāh may forgive disobedience to some of His commands, or He may punish the believer by causing him to stay for an appropriate period in Hell. But after that term, Allāh, in His mercy, grants Paradise.

exchanged for this other abode (i. e., Paradise]." When the soul sees what is in Paradise, he cries, "My Lord, hasten the arrival of the Hour [i. e., the Resurrection] so that I maybe joined with my family and wealth." Thereupon it is said to him, "Rest in tranquillity."'

Allāh's Messenger (ﷺ) continued, 'When the disbelieving servant [and in another narration "sinful servant"] is about to leave this world and enter the next, angels,[93] powerful and severe, descend to him from the heavens - their faces black and carrying with them coarse strips of cloth from Hell. They sit before him at a distance as far as the eye can see. Then the Angel of Death arrives, and sitting at the head of the disbeliever, he says, "O you foul soul, come out to the anger and wrath of your Lord." The soul inside the disbeliever's body is overcome by terrible fear [and does not want to deliver itself up], whereupon the Angel of Death violently pulls it out like multi-pronged skewers being yanked out of wet wool - tearing with them the arteries and nerves. Upon this, the soul is cursed by every angel between the earth and the heavens and by those inside the heavens. Then the doors of the heavens are closed to him, and every single guard at these doors begs Allāh that this soul not be carried up in front of him.' The Prophet (ﷺ) continued, 'The Angel of Death barely receives the soul in his hands, whereupon the other angels grasp it from him and wrap it up in coarse cloth. There emits from it the foulest odour that could be found on the face of the earth. They ascend with it, never passing a host of angels without being asked, "Who is this ugly soul?" They reply, "So and so, the son of so and so," using the worst names by which he was known in this world. When they arrive at the lowest heaven, they request that it be opened for this soul, but the request is denied.' At this point Allāh's Messenger (ﷺ) recited the verse: 'The gates of the heavens will not be opened for them, nor will they enter the Garden of Paradise until a camel goes

[93] As mentioned in authentic narrations of Aḥmad, these are the "angels of torment."

through the eye of a needle.'[94] After that he continued, 'Then Allāh, the Mighty and Majestic, says [to the angels], "Place his record in *sijjīn*[95] - in the lowest earth. Return My servant to the earth, for verily I have promised mankind that having created them from the earth, I will return them to it. And I will make them come out of it, yet another time." Upon this command, the deceased [disbeliever's] soul is thrown down from the sky until it lands in its body.' The Prophet (ﷺ) then recited the verse: 'And whoever ascribes partners with Allāh, it is as though he had fallen from the sky, such that birds snatch him up or the wind throws him to a remote place.'[96] Then he commented, 'Verily [when the soul is returned to its body], the deceased hears the sound of his companions' footsteps as they turn away from his grave.' [The Prophet (ﷺ) resumed his explanation, saying], 'Then two angels, severe in interrogation, come to him, and sitting him up, they begin to question him, "Who is your Lord?" He replies, "Hah! Hah![97] I don't know," They continue by asking him, "What is your religion?" He answers, "Hah! Hah! I don't know," So they ask, "Then what do you say about this man who was sent to you?" [The disbeliever does not appear to understand who they are referring to, so it is said], "Muḥammad." Again he states, "Hah! Hah! I don't know. I only heard people talking about him." Then it is said, "You did not know! And you did not read!"[98] Thereupon a voice from the heavens is

---

[94] Sūrah *al-A'rāf,* 7:40.

[95] According to commentators, "*sijjīn*" refers to the book which contains all of the deeds of the devils and the disbelievers. See al-Alusi's *Rūḥ al-Ma'ānī* vol. 30, p. 71. It is said that *sijjeen* is a place below the seventh earth - the place of Iblees and his forces. For details, see *Tafsīr al-Jalālayn*, p. 789.

[96] Sūrah *al-Ḥajj*, 22:31.

[97] Usually, this expression describes a state of surprise, shock, pain or amusement. However, in this context, it can only refer to the first three.

[98] This refers to the Qur'ān, which is available to all who wish to read it and benefit from its guidance. In a wider sense, it could refer to the reading of literature on Islāmic teachings which invite to the truth.

heard, "He has lied! So spread out for him a place from the Fire and open for him a window to the Fire." The searing hot winds of Hell engulf him while his grave closes in upon him, crushing him until his ribcage is broken by the force -causing the ribs of one side to intertwine with the ribs of the other. Then there appears to him a person with an ugly face and ugly clothing and exuding a foul odour, who says, "Tidings of evil to you, for this is the day which you were promised!" The deceased says to him, "And you, too; may Allāh give you evil tidings! Who are you, for yours is a face which portends evil." The person rejoins, "I represent your wicked deeds. By Allāh, I have always known you to be slow in obedience to Allāh and quick in disobedience to Him. May Allāh reward you with evil." Then one who is deaf, dumb and blind[99] and is carrying an iron rod is sent to the deceased. If he were to strike a mountain with it, the mountain would disintegrate into rubble. He strikes the deceased with a blow which turns him into dust. Allāh returns the deceased to his original form, whereupon he is struck a second time. This causes him to shriek with such violence that it is heard by all of creation except mankind and *jinn*. Then a door to the Fire is opened, and beddings of the Fire are spread for him, whereupon he cries, "Lord, do not establish the Hour!"[100]

---

[99] Perhaps the reason for this type of figure is that it represents a severe form of rebuke to both the deceased *ḳāfir* and the deceased, disobedient and hypocritical Muslim who did not practice his religion. It is an appropriate symbol as it signifies his spiritual circumstances on earth - deaf, dumb and blind.

[100] The disbelievers, hypocrites and sinful Muslims do not want the establishment of the last Hour and subsequently, the Resurrection and Judgement. The disbelievers and the hypocrites are doomed to endless torment in the Hellfire. Sinful Muslims who maintained correct beliefs (affirming *tawḥīd*) are also liable for a term of punishment in the Hellfire (may Allāh protect us from it) but by Allāh's mercy may enter Heaven at a later time.

The Meeting of Souls

Souls of the Dead Meeting with Each Other

The souls of the dead may be divided into the following two categories: (a) favoured souls (those of pious believers) and (b) punished souls (those of sinful believers and disbelievers). The souls of the second group are confined to places of punishment and are too preoccupied with the torments of the gave to be able to meet or visit with each other. However, the blessed and favoured souls of the pious believers are free to roam and meet. They may visit and discuss with each other their previous existence on earth. In the *barzakh* every soul will be with companions of like nature.[101]

In his book, *Kitāb al-Rūḥ*,[102] Ibn al-Qayyim supports this view by bringing proof from the Qur'ān and the sunnah. He also relates experiences of various scholars regarding what they were informed of in dreams by the souls of their pious, departed companions. The *sharī'ah* cannot be based upon the latter, for it is a matter which only the texts of divine revelation can decide. However, there are texts which indirectly give support to Ibn al-Qayyim's assertions as well as those which are obviously clearer in nature.[103]

---

[101] Ibn al-Qayyim's *Kitāb al-Rūḥ*, p. 28 and al-Ālūsī's *al-Āyāt al-Bayyināt* p. 106.

[102] See pp. 28-32.

[103] These clear references are discussed in the chapter entitled "The Soul's Abode Between Death and the Resurrection."

The following is a sample of a text whose statement is indirect in nature:

عن مسروق قال: قال أصحاب محمد (ﷺ): ما ينبغي لنا أن نفارقك في الدنيا، فإذا مت رفعت فوقنا فلم نرك. فأنزل الله تعالى: ﴿وَمَن يُطِعِ اللَّهَ وَالرَّسُولَ فَأُوْلَـٰئِكَ مَعَ الَّذِينَ أَنْعَمَ اللَّهُ عَلَيْهِم مِّنَ النَّبِيِّينَ وَالصِّدِّيقِينَ وَالشُّهَدَاءِ وَالصَّالِحِينَ وَحَسُنَ أُولَـٰئِكَ رَفِيقًا﴾

> Masrūq reported "The companions said to the Messenger of Allāh (ﷺ), 'We must not part company with you in this world[104] because when you die and are raised up above, we will not be able to see you.' Then Allāh, the Exalted, revealed the following verse: 'Whoever obeys Allāh and the Messenger will be in the company of those whom Allāh has shown favour- the prophets, the affirmers of truth,[105] the martyrs and the righteous. What a wonderful company they are!'" [106]

According to Ibn al-Qayyim, this "company" or "fellowship" is established in the *dunyā* and is resumed in the *barzakh* and in the Hereafter. Man is with whom he loves in these three stages of the soul's existence. The souls of faithful believers join the messengers and prophets of Allāh, along with the affirmers of truth, the martyrs and the pious. This blissful fellowship is not restricted to the Hereafter (i.e., Paradise) but begins immediately after death in the *barzakh*.

---

[104] Their extreme love and affection for the Prophet (ﷺ) made them feel that they never wanted to part from his company.

[105] The word "*ṣiddīqūn*" ("affirmers of truth") denotes very pious people (like Abū Bakr al-Ṣiddiq) who firmly and steadfastly testify to the truth and who are unwavering in support of it.

[106] This tradition is mursal (the companion has not been named in the *isnād*), but its chain of transmitters is dependable. See *Kitāb al-Rūḥ*, p. 28, footnote 2. The Qur'ānic reference is Sūrah *al-Nisā'*, 4:69.

The following text is a direct reference to this point and clear proof that, in general, the souls of pious believers are able to meet and converse with each other:

عن أبي هريرة (رضي الله عنه) أن رسول الله (ﷺ) قال: إن المؤمن يصعد بروحه إلى السماء فتأتيه أرواح المؤمنين فيستخبرون عن معارفهم من أهل الأرض

Abū Hurayrah reported that Allāh's Messenger (ﷺ) said: "Verily, the soul of the believer [after death] soars up to the heavens, whereupon the souls of other believers come to it, seeking news about those they know from the people of the earth."[107]

Souls of the Dead Meeting with Souls of the Sleeping

Is it possible that the souls of the dead and the living meet with each other and converse? If so, how does such a thing occur? These and other questions are often asked regarding the nature of souls, their powers and their influence. In his treatise on the soul, Ibn al-Qayyim proves that it is possible and, in fact, occurs. He draws on his understanding of the Qur'ān and considers the opinions and experiences of the pious predecessors regarding this issue. He also applies logic and reasoning to prove his position. In order to arrive at the most dependable conclusion, it is essential to critically analyze and evaluate the proofs he and others[108] use.

---

[107] Authenticated by al-Suyūṭī and affirmed by Nāṣiruddeen al-Albānī in his book, *Silsilat al-Aḥādīth al-Ṣaḥīḥah*, ḥadīth no. 2628. See *al-Āyāt al-Bayyināt* , p. 105, footnote 2.

[108] Such as Ibn Mandah in his *Kitāb al-Nafs wa al-Rūḥ*, Abū Bakr bin Marwān al-Mālikī in his *Kitāb al-Mujālasah*, and al-Ālūsī in his *Rūḥ al-Maʿānī*.

Ibn al-Qayyim's first source is the Qur'ān, specifically the verses which refer to the condition of the soul during sleep and death:

ٱللَّهُ يَتَوَفَّى ٱلْأَنفُسَ حِينَ مَوْتِهَا وَٱلَّتِى
لَمْ تَمُتْ فِى مَنَامِهَا ۖ فَيُمْسِكُ ٱلَّتِى قَضَىٰ عَلَيْهَا ٱلْمَوْتَ
وَيُرْسِلُ ٱلْأُخْرَىٰٓ إِلَىٰٓ أَجَلٍ مُّسَمًّى

> "Allāh takes souls at the time of their death and [the souls] of those that do not die during their sleep. He retains those souls for which He has ordained death, whereas He releases the rest for an appointed term."[109]

Ibn al-Qayyim mentions two viewpoints regarding the *tafsīr* on this verse. The first view has been previously stated but will be repeated for the purpose of comparison. It asserts that there are two points in time at which Allāh takes souls: at death and during sleep. Death may occur during sleep or at other times. The soul taken at death is the "retained"[110] soul referred to in this verse. The "released" soul is that which is taken during sleep and is returned to its respective body upon awakening.

The second position in regard to this verse is that both the "retained" soul and the "released" one are taken during sleep. Then those who have completed their specified period of life are retained, while those who have not completed their time are returned to their bodies. This view suggests that the verse refers to only the souls that die in their sleep and the souls which are returned to their respective bodies upon awakening, and does not mention the "retained" souls that die at times other than during sleep.

---

[109] Sūrah *al-Zumar*, 39:42.

[110] It is retained until the Day of Resurrection, when the soul is reunited in life with the body. However, the soul is also returned to the body for the questioning in the grave by the two angels, Munkar and Nakīr, and for the term of its torment in the grave, if decreed. However, these restricted and particular types of "returning" of the soul to the body do not result in the resumption of normal earthly life.

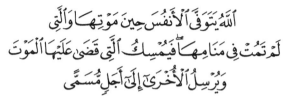

Ibn al-Qayyim provides a long argument in defense of the first viewpoint even in contradiction to his respected mentor and teacher, Shaykh al-Islām Ibn Taymiyyah.[111]

Since the souls of the living (which are sleeping) and the souls of the dead can roam in the spiritual world - for they are not tied to their earthly bodies - it is certainly possible that they meet and converse. This deduction is confirmed by the majority of dependable Qur'ānic commentators, foremost among them, Imām Ibn Jarīr al-Ṭabarī and Ibn Kathīr. The former mentions the following *tafsīr* of the above-stated verse: "Allāh, the Exalted, indicates that the souls of the living [which are sleeping] and the souls of the dead meet during sleep, when visions occur in dreams. Thus, those whom Allāh wills meet with one another. He detains the souls of the dead, while releasing the souls of the living back to their bodies until the appointed time when death has been ordained for them."[112] Ibn Kathīr states in his *tafsīr*: "In this verse is proof that the souls of the living [which are sleeping] and the souls of the dead meet in a host of the upper heights [i.e., the heavens]."[113]

In support of the view that the souls of the living (which are sleeping) can meet and converse with the souls of the dead, all of the aforementioned scholars refer to the following narration:

عن ابن عباس قال: بلغني أن أرواح الأحياء والأموات تلتقي في المنام، فيتساءلون بينهم، فيمسك الله أرواح الموتى، ويرسل أرواح الأحياء إلى أجسادها

It is reported that Ibn 'Abbās said. "I have been informed that the souls of the living [which are sleeping] and the souls of

[111] See *Kitāb al-Rūḥ*, pp. 34-35.

[112] See al-Ṭabarī's *Jāmi' al-Bayān 'an Ta' wīl Āyāt al-Qur'ān*, vol. 24, pp. 8-9.

[113] See *Tafsīr al-Qur'ān al-'Aẓīm*, vol. 7, p. 92.

> the dead meet during sleep, and they question each other. Then Allāh detains the souls of the dead and releases the souls of the living to return to their bodies."[114]

Although its context substantiates their interpretation of the Qur'ānic verse, this narration is not dependable from the perspective of its *isnād*. In fact, stringent research has not furnished any pertinent texts from the authentic sunnah which relate clearly to this particular issue.

Notwithstanding the aforementioned Qur'ānic verse, the strongest arguments in favour of the possibility of the souls of the living (which are sleeping) and the souls of the dead meeting are drawn from the actual observations and reports affirming such phenomena. These reports - as single isolated incidents - are no proof in themselves; however, when taken as a whole, their overwhelming number and dependable sources are impossible to deny. One can safely and sensibly refer to their countless occurrences all over the world as additional evidence to be considered alongside other clearer and more firmly established proof.[115] Ibn al-Qayyim quotes a good number of these reports recounting certain pious individuals' personal experiences which occurred during their sleep - in the realm of visions. [116]

Ibn al-Qayyim's strongest arguments in support of this issue are based on logic and rational thought. It is centered on such

---

114 This *athar* (narration on the authority of a companion) has been related by Ibn Mandah, Ibn Jarīr, et. al. However, it has been deemed weak due to the presence of fault in one of its transmitters, Ja'far bin Abul Mugheerah. For details, see lbn Ḥajar's *Tahdhīb al-Tabdhīb* and al-Dhahabī's *Mīzān al-I' tidāl*, under the entry "Ja'far."

115 See al-Safārīnī's *Lawāmi' al-Anwār*, vol. 2, p. 58.

116 Whoever wishes to delve deeper into this particular subject may read these reports in his *Kitāb al-Rūḥ*. See especially pp. 35-50. However, the reader should be warned that none of these stories bear a dependable *isnād* traced to their final narrator. It is only as a whole that they may be taken to indicate secondary evidence in support of this issue as a valid concept.

observable, undeniable data as the aforementioned. He argues that the occurrence of a meeting between the souls of the living (which are sleeping) and the souls of the dead is proven by the fact that a living person, for example, sees a dead personality in dreams and asks him information about a certain matter of which the former was in complete ignorance. Thereupon, he is informed by the deceased person and finds the information to be true, regardless of whether it was an event of the past or the future. Sometimes, the soul of the dead person informs him about money or goods hidden or buried in a certain place known only to the deceased. Or the deceased may inform him regarding a certain debt owed, along with minute details of its circumstances and conditions. Ibn al-Qayyim points out even more amazing phenomena, such as the deceased soul informing the soul of the sleeping person regarding a deed performed by the latter which he has never disclosed to anyone else! What could be more astounding than the deceased's soul informing the living person's soul about personal affairs of the latter which the living person is certain that none but himself knows about?! [117]

One might dispute the significance of visions or dreams which occur during sleep. It might be argued that the sleeper experiencing such "visions" merely sees a series of "moving" pictures or illustrations which reflect inner beliefs, fears, preoccupations, etc. Ibn al-Qayyim admits that this is true in many circumstances, but he directs attention to the fact that visions[118] are of three kinds: those from Allāh, those from Satan[119] and those from the soul conversing with itself. Moreover, there are various categories of true visions. Among these is *ilhām* (inspiration) - Allāh's words

---

[117] Abridged from *Kitāb al-Rūḥ*, p. 35.

[118] A vision during sleep is termed "*ru'yā*," literally, "a thing seen," for one "sees" certain things during sleep.

[119] Actually, according to authentic traditions related by al-Bukhārī and Muslim, the "*ru'yā*" ("vision") is from Allāh, whereas that from Satan . is termed "*aḥlām*" ("dreams").

spoken into the heart of the believer during sleep.[120] Another type is *mathal* (likeness or parable, which is conveyed to the sleeper by the angel of visions assigned to him. A third kind consists of the sleeper's soul meeting with the souls of the dead, such as his family, relatives, companions and others as mentioned earlier.[121]

Souls of the Sleeping Conversing with Each Other

Since the previously quoted Qur'ānic verse clarifies that human souls leave the body[122] during sleep to roam about in the spiritual realm, and it has been established that they can meet the souls of the dead, then it is logical to assume that they are able to meet each other as well. Ibn al-Qayyim confirms this point and replies to the following often-posed question of doubt: "How does a person during sleep 'see' himself conversing with other living people, even though they are far away and awake - their souls having not left their bodies?" How do their souls "meet" per se? Ibn al-Qayyim answers that this phenomenon is either a likeness (*mathal*) made for the soul of the sleeper by the angel of visions or a result of the sleeper's soul conversing with itself (*ḥadīthu nafs*). This "conversation" is illustrated in the images seen in his dreams.[123]

Souls of the Dead Meeting with People Who are Awake

It is a common concept among some people and cultures that the souls of the dead can and do come back to the earth

---

[120] As has been said by the companion, 'Ubādah bin al-Ṣāmiṭ.

[121] Abridged from *Kitāb al-Rūḥ*, pp. 44-45.

[122] This is a partial separation (*juz'ī*) and not the complete separation (*kulli*), whose effect is death.

[123] See *Kitāb al-Rūḥ*, pp. 47-48.

and converse with the living (who are awake). In order to assess the validity of such a claim it is essential to explore the various literature relating to this issue.

From the sources available, research can only lead to a conclusion that it is neither possible nor proven that the souls of the dead return to the world of the living, meet with them, converse and so on. This conclusion is based on the texts of the divinely revealed law, and the following evidence from the Qur'ān and the sunnah clearly affirms such a stand.

Evidence from the Qur'ān Against Return

There are a number of Qur'ānic verses whose texts unequivocally prove that the souls of the dead do not return to the earth. For the sake of brevity only two are quoted, the first as follows:

حَتَّىٰٓ إِذَا جَآءَ أَحَدَهُمُ ٱلْمَوْتُ قَالَ رَبِّ
ٱرْجِعُونِ ﴿٩٩﴾ لَعَلِّىٓ أَعْمَلُ صَٰلِحًا فِيمَا تَرَكْتُ ۚ كَلَّآ ۚ إِنَّهَا كَلِمَةٌ
هُوَ قَآئِلُهَا ۖ وَمِن وَرَآئِهِم بَرْزَخٌ إِلَىٰ يَوْمِ يُبْعَثُونَ ﴿١٠٠﴾

> "[The disbelievers persist in their rejection of the truth of the Resurrection][124] until when death comes to one of them, he says, 'My Lord, send me back [to life] so that I may work in righteousness regarding things left behind.' But no! It is only a word he says; and behind them is a barrier until the day they are raised up."[125]

In these verses Allāh describes the condition of the disbelieving polytheists who reject the existence of the Resurrection and who say:

---

[124] This phrase is understood; these verses continue a line of argumentation begun in the preceding verses.

[125] Sūrah *al-Mu'minūn*, 23:99-100.

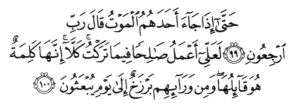

قَالُوٓا۟ أَءِذَا مِتْنَا وَكُنَّا تُرَابًا وَعِظَٰمًا أَءِنَّا لَمَبْعُوثُونَ ﴿٨٢﴾ لَقَدْ وُعِدْنَا نَحْنُ وَءَابَآؤُنَا هَٰذَا مِن قَبْلُ إِنْ هَٰذَآ إِلَّآ أَسَٰطِيرُ ٱلْأَوَّلِينَ ﴿٨٣﴾

> "If we become dust and bones, are we to be resurrected?! We and our forefathers before us have been promised this already. Such is nothing but fables of the ancients!"[126]

But when death comes upon one of them he realizes his misguidance and error; when he sees the Angel of Death approaching to seize his soul he wishes he could return to life to rectify his rejection of the truth and perform works of piety. But the reply is an emphatic "No!" His petitioning for a return to earth is not going to be answered.[127] The fact that he cannot return to the earth is finalized by the statement that a barrier (*barzakh*) has been erected behind him and thus he cannot return to any other existence in the world.[128] The word "*barzakh*" is used here to indicate a veil, barrier or partition between two things.[129] According to Qur'ānic commentators, the *barzakh* is the barrier between death and any return to worldly existence. This has also been related by *Mujāhid*,[130] one of the dependable scholars of *tafsīr*. The great commentator and companion, Ibn ʿAbbās, defines it as a *ḥijāb* (a partition or veil). Al-Ḍaḥḥāk, another *tābiʿī* scholar of *tafsīr*, says that the *barzakh* is the stage between this world and

---

126 Sūrah *al-Mu'minūn*, 23:82-83.

127 See al-Qurṭubī's *al-Jāmiʿu li Aḥkām al-Qur'ān*, vol. 12, p. 150.

128 This is a clear refutation of the false claims of certain philosophers and proponents of various religions which adhere to a belief in the transmigration of souls or in reincarnation.

129 See al-Iṣfahānī's *Muʿjam Mufradāt Alfādh al-Qur'ān*, p. 41 and Ibn al-Athīr's *al-Nihāyah fī Gharīb al-Ḥadīth* vol. 1, p. 118.

130 A *tābiʿī*.

the Hereafter.[131] In his *tafsīr*, al-Qurṭubī concludes his exposition of these various interpretations, stating, "The *barzakh* is a barrier between two things. It is the stage between this world and the other world -from the time of death until the Resurrection. Thus, whoever dies enters the *barzakh*."[132] There are no contradictions among the various explanations by these scholars; rather, they all point to one undeniable fact: the soul, having been separated from its earthly body, enters into a realm behind which there is a barrier prohibiting any return.

Some may argue that the above-mentioned verses refer to only the stubborn rejecters of truth, such as polytheists and other disbelievers who deny the Resurrection and Judgement. On that assumption, Muslims and those from other faiths and philosophies who believe in the Resurrection are not indicated by these Qur'ānic verses. However, although these verses specifically refer to the polytheists of Makkah (who denied the possibility of the resurrection of the soul), it includes all souls of the dead, regardless of who they are. This is affirmed by a second Qur'ānic text which follows:

يَٰٓأَيُّهَا ٱلَّذِينَ ءَامَنُوا۟ لَا تُلْهِكُمْ
أَمْوَٰلُكُمْ وَلَآ أَوْلَٰدُكُمْ عَن ذِكْرِ ٱللَّهِ ۚ وَمَن يَفْعَلْ
ذَٰلِكَ فَأُو۟لَٰٓئِكَ هُمُ ٱلْخَٰسِرُونَ ﴿٩﴾ وَأَنفِقُوا۟ مِن مَّا رَزَقْنَٰكُم
مِّن قَبْلِ أَن يَأْتِىَ أَحَدَكُمُ ٱلْمَوْتُ فَيَقُولَ رَبِّ لَوْلَآ أَخَّرْتَنِىٓ
إِلَىٰٓ أَجَلٍ قَرِيبٍ فَأَصَّدَّقَ وَأَكُن مِّنَ ٱلصَّٰلِحِينَ ﴿١٠﴾ وَلَن
يُؤَخِّرَ ٱللَّهُ نَفْسًا إِذَا جَآءَ أَجَلُهَا ۚ وَٱللَّهُ خَبِيرٌۢ بِمَا تَعْمَلُونَ ﴿١١﴾

"O you who believe, do not let your wealth and children distract you from the remembrance[133] of Allāh. Those of you

---

[131] See al-Qurṭubī's *tafsīr*, Vol12, p. 150.

[132] Ibid.

[133] Indicates all duties towards Allāh, such as prayer, fasting, charity, etc.

> who do so are the losers. And spend in charity something from that which We have provided you before death comes to one of you, whereupon he says, 'My Lord, if only You would grant me respite for a while, so I could give alms and be among the righteous.' But Allāh will never grant reprieve to any soul when its appointed time has come. And Allāh is aware of all that you do."[134]

In these verses Allāh, the Blessed and Exalted, warns the believers not to be diverted from their duties and obligations to their Creator due to being engrossed in their wealth and offspring. Furthermore, they are encouraged to give charity from the sustenance which has been provided by their gracious Lord. It is emphasized that they must do this before death comes, at which time one will wish to be granted another term of life - if only just a little while - in order to perform righteous deeds. Ibn 'Abbās, denying that return is refused only to disbelievers, recited these verses which indicate the deceased believer's soul requesting a return to the world in order to do works of righteousness.[135]

Evidence from the Sunnah Against Return

There are a number of texts from the sunnah which further support the contention that even the pious and most righteous believers' souls cannot return to the earth. One example is sufficient to prove the point. As it is well known, the souls of Muslim martyrs are freed upon death to roam in Paradise to partake of some of its pleasure in a limited fashion. The following tradition relates that the martyr desires to return to the world but cannot:

قال النبي (ﷺ): ما من عبد يموت، له عند الله خير، يحب أن
يرجع إلى الدنيا وأن له الدنيا وما فيها، إلا الشهيد، لما يرى من
فضل الشهادة فإنه يحب أن يرجع إلى الدنيا فيقتل مرة أخرى

---

[134] Sūrah *al-Munāfiqūn*, 63:9-11.

[135] See al-Qurṭubī's *tafsīr* Vol. 18, pp. 130-131.

> The Prophet (ﷺ) said. "No servant who has good in store for him with Allāh and dies ever wants to return to the earth - even if he were to have the whole world and everything that is in it - except for the martyr. And that is due to what he sees in the nobility of martyrdom. Verily, he would like to return back to the earth in order to be martyred another time."[136]

The preceding texts of both the Qur'ān and the sunnah clearly illustrate that the souls of the dead do not come back to the earth to visit relatives or friends, neither in the form of a spirit or an apparition,[137] nor in their previous bodies[138] or in any other person's body.[139]

Various Philosophies Supporting the Return of the Soul

The belief in the transmigration of souls is an ancient concept held by certain sects of Hinduism, Buddhism and some philosophical schools of Greece and Persia. Certain Muslim thinkers were greatly influenced by such concepts due to the translation of the religious and philosophical works of Greece, India and Persia during the Abbasid reign. Since the philosophies of such foreign sources completely contradicted, purely authentic Islāmic teachings, the majority of scholars and laymen rejected them. However, these systems did have some influence on certain people weak in faith and weak in the knowledge of the proven Islāmic sciences based upon the texts of the divinely revealed *sharī'ah*. Thus, there exist various philosophers, such as Ibn

---

136 Authentically related by al-Tirmidhī, Muslim, et. al.

137 Such as a glowing form resembling a human.

138 Because they are subject to decay and decomposition.

139 Such as is alleged by Buddhists or philosophers who say that a transmigration of souls occurs. Others claim that the deceased person's soul may enter a live person's body and use it as a medium with which to communicate with the living.

Sīnā'[140] and a group of Bāṭinite[141] thinkers called "*Ikhwān al-Ṣafā*,"[142] who support positions, contrary to Islāmic teachings. It is from such deviated "thinkers" that one hears certain untenable views regarding the soul.

These philosophers claim that "when 'perfect' souls leave their loved ones in this world, they busy themselves helping the 'incomplete' souls [confined to their bodies on the earth] escape from their 'lesser' condition and rise to a much higher and more noble level."[143] According to their view, the souls of the dead appear to the living on the earth and converse with them with the objective of "educating" them and "polishing" their "confined" souls.[144]

---

[140] He was born in 370 A.H./980 A.D. in Khurāsān and died in Iraq in 428 AR/1037 A.D. In the West, he is most famous for his books on medicine and other sciences, especially philosophy and logic. For details of his life and works, see al-Dhahabī's *Siyar Aʿlām al-Nubalā'*, vol. 17, pp. 531-536. In his magnificent refutation entitled *Daru Taʿārudh al-ʿAql wan-Naql*, Shaykh al-Islām Ibn Taymiyyah gives a detailed account of Ibn Sīnā's errors and misguidance in matters of faith due to the strong influence of Greek' philosophy. See vol. 1, pp. 9-11.

[141] The name given to those sects which hold that the texts of the divine *sharīʿah* have an outer, surface aspect (*dhāhir*) and an inner, deeper meaning (*bāṭin*). In order to suit their own whims and distorted, preconceived notions, they allege that the surface aspect is known and followed by the masses while the inner aspect is known to them alone. See al-Ghazālī's *Faḍā'iḥ al-Bāṭiniyyah* and al-Khaṭib's *al-Ḥarakāt al-Bāṭiniyyah fil Ālam al-Islāmī*.

[142] A group of philosophers who were, in reality, Ismāʿīlī Bāṭinites. They drew on ancient philosophies of Greece and Persia. See al-Nashshār's *Nash'at al-Fikr al-Falsafī fil Islām*, vol. 2, pp. 289-297.

[143] See p. 133 of the dissertation, "*al-ʿIlal wal-Maʿlūlāt*" from their *Rasāil Ikhwān al-Ṣafā*, as reported in Ṭanṭāwī Jawharī's Qur'ānic commentary, *al-Jawāhir fī Tafsīr al-Qur'ān*, vol. 9, p. 102.

[144] See *al-Jawāhir*, vol. 9, p. 102.

Among the Modernist[145] scholars who avidly support this view is the Egyptian philosopher, Ṭanṭāwī Jawharī. He dedicates many pages of his "scientific" *tafsīr* to expounding the reports and experiences of various individuals who had delved into the practice of attempting to bring dead souls back to this world in order to converse with them. He is so enthralled by the idea that he claims that "there is a unanimous consensus from both the West and the East, science and religion, that the souls of the dead make contact with living people of this world. These souls resemble devils at certain times, while upon other occasions they resemble angels. The 'complete' [or 'perfect'] soul among these teaches the living and guides them on the straight path."[146]

It is incumbent to reply to such a bold and erroneous statement which represents nothing more than the author's empty claim. His statement that there is unanimous agreement from the scholars of the East and West in the disciplines of science and religion regarding the return of souls to the earth is a gross exaggeration of facts. The believers of such a theory are a minority in the West and consist of a fringe group that loves to delve in the mystical, exotic, strange and bizarre. Such a thing does not exist among the Islāmic people of the East, for they have been blessed and illuminated by the divine *sharī'ah*.

Furthermore, neither established science nor revealed religion supports Jawharī's inflated allegation which is based upon mere conjecture. As the Qur'ān states:

---

[145] The past century has produced a movement which has been termed by some as "Modernist." It is characterised by so-called "new research" in Islamic studies which claims to be critical and scientific. In reality, it depends heavily upon personal opinion, rationalism and extensive borrowing from systems and philosophies foreign to Islām. It has Produced the likes of Muḥammad 'Abduh (Jawharī's teacher), Muḥammad Haykal, Ṭā Hā Ḥusayn, Fareed Wajdī, et. al.

[146] See *al-Jawāhir*, vol. 9, p. 102.

وَإِنَّ ٱلظَّنَّ لَا يُغْنِى مِنَ ٱلْحَقِّ شَيْـًٔا

"Conjecture avails nothing against the truth."[147]

Moreover, the Prophet (ﷺ) warned us:

إياكم والظن فإن الظن أكذب الحديث

"Beware of mere conjecture, for verily, conjecture is the most deceptive of all thought."[148]

In order to refute and prove the error of his unfounded claims, it is essential to scrutinize what Ṭanṭāwī Jawharī has presented as evidence in an attempt to substantiate his position regarding this issue. His "evidence" is from three sources: the Torah,[149] a few Qur'ānic verses, and observations and reports of certain strange phenomena which he interprets to indicate the return of souls from the dead to visit the living (who are awake) on this earth.

Alleged Evidence from the Torah and its Refutation

Ṭanṭāwī Jawharī uses the story of Saul in the First Book of Samuel as evidence of the possibility of souls of the dead returning to the world of the living. The Biblical story relates that having grown old, Samuel (a prophet according to Christian and Jewish lore) appointed his sons as judges over Israel. However, because they were corrupt, the people demanded that Samuel select a new king to rule over them like other nations. So Samuel appointed

---

[147] Sūrah *al-Najm*, 53:28.

[148] Authentically related by al-Bukhārī and Muslim.

[149] The present day Torah is merely remnants of texts claimed to have been revealed to Moses (upon whom be peace). These are the first five books of the Bible, termed the "Pentateuch." These are not revealed words of Allāh, but rather, historical narratives related by early chroniclers. These texts have been subjected to gross alterations and interpolations and cannot be depended upon. For detailed proof of such distortions, contradictions, errors and alterations, see Maurice Bucaille's treatise, The Bible, the Qur'ān and Science, pp. 4-43.

Saul, but Saul was also corrupt, which invited the wrath of God.[150] When Samuel died, all of Israel lamented the passing of their spiritual leader. At that time the Philistines gathered their armies for war against Israel. King Saul also gathered his army of Israelites, but when he saw the host of Philistines, he was afraid and his heart greatly trembled. He prayed unto the Lord but was not answered, neither by way of a prophet being sent nor by dreams.

At that point Saul ordered his servants to seek a conjuress of spirits, saying to them, "Seek me a woman that hath a familiar spirit so that I may go to her and inquire of her."[151] When the woman was found, Saul inquired, "I pray thee, divine unto me by the familiar spirit and bring me him up, whom I shall name unto thee." The conjuress asked Saul who it was that she should bring up from the dead, to which he replied, "Samuel." The woman brought up the soul of Samuel, an old man covered in a mantle, whereupon Saul stooped with his face to the ground, bowing himself before the apparition.[152] At that point the soul of Samuel conversed with King Saul, saying, "Why hast thou disquieted me to bring me up?"[153] Saul replied that he had called upon him due to his distress that the Philistines were making war against him and that, God no longer heard him. He requested Samuel to advise him as to what to do. Samuel rebuked Saul for asking him since God had forsaken Saul and had become his enemy; yet Samuel still informed Saul that the Lord had taken his kingship from him and had given it to David[154] as a punishment for not obeying His commands. Samuel further

---

[150] See I Samuel, 8, 10, 13-15 and 17-18.

[151] See I Samuel, 28:7.

[152] See I Samuel, 28:8-14.

[153] That is, to bring his soul from the dead.

[154] The champion of the Philistines, the youth who slew Goliath by firing a stone from his slingshot. According to The First Book of Samuel, Saul was exceedingly jealous of David, who had become a national hero. Saul even tried to have David murdered by any means at his disposal.

prophesised that the Lord would deliver Saul and Israel into the hands of the Philistines and that the next day Saul and his sons would be with him (i.e., Samuel).[155] Upon hearing that, King Saul swooned and fell to the ground unconscious.[156] Samuel's prophecy came to pass, for the Philistines fought a violent war against Israel in which Saul's sons were killed and he was badly wounded. Not wanting to be taken prisoner by the Philistines, Saul threw himself upon his sword and perished.[157]

The aforementioned passage, alleged to be from the Torah and thus attributed to Prophet Moses (peace be upon him), is not even part of the extant remnants of the Torah. What actually remains are the first five books of the Old Testament (beginning with Genesis and ending with Deuteronomy). Since Moses' death is reported in Deuteronomy and Samuel existed much later than that, it is obvious that Moses could not have written the later books of the Old Testament. Thus, Jawharī commits a gross error by attributing the story of Samuel to the Torah and, by implication, to Moses. Obviously, this story forms a part of the later additions and alterations to the Torah by the Old Testament chroniclers. Since the Old Testament has fallen prey to such obvious human distortions and interpolations, it cannot be relied upon as a source of dependably related information.

In addition, the story of Saul has definite contradictions and elements of untruth which prove that human hands have altered and distorted it. In the beginning of chapter 9 of I Samuel, it is said of Saul that he was not corrupt, but rather, "there was not among the Children of Israel a goodlier person than he."[158] Furthermore, in chapter 10 he was told by Samuel that God had chosen him as

---

155 This is a prophecy about their approaching deaths.

156 See I Samuel, 28:15-18.

157 See I Samuel, 31:1-6.

158 I Samuel, 9:2.

"captain over His inheritance,"[159] that "the Spirit of the Lord" would come upon him,[160] and that he could do as occasion served him, for God was with him.[161] The Qur'ān confirms the righteousness of Ṭālūt (Saul)[162] and mentions that a prophet from the Children of Israel informed the Israelites that Allāh had appointed Ṭālūt as king over them.[163] The Children of Israel complained about this choice, claiming that he was not deserving of the kingship since he was not gifted with an abundance of wealth. Thereupon that prophet replied to the Israelites:

قَالَ إِنَّ ٱللَّهَ ٱصْطَفَىٰهُ
عَلَيْكُمْ وَزَادَهُۥ بَسْطَةً فِى ٱلْعِلْمِ وَٱلْجِسْمِ

"Verily, Allāh has chosen him above you and has increased him abundantly in knowledge, bodily stature and prowess."[164]

In contrast to this favourable character description, Biblical narrative also portrays Saul as devoid of moral qualities. According to the picture painted by the chroniclers of the Bible, he goes from the "goodliest of people" to one of the worst. This noble and virtuous Saul, who was chosen by God above the other Children of Israel to be their king, who had the "spirit" of God with him, etc., is painted as a treacherous, envious person who lusts for the blood of his own son-in-law, David. He is depicted as a desperate man who, being deserted by God and losing all faith in Him, plunges on his sword in suicide!

This is a clear example of the many instances of the Biblical narratives being tampered with and distorted by the Jewish

---

159 I Samuel, 10:1.

160 I Samuel, 10:6.

161 I Samuel, 10:7.

162 A brief outline of his story is mentioned in Sūrah *al-Baqarah* 2:246-251.

163 See Sūrah *al-Baqarah*, 2:247.

164 Sūrah *al-Baqarah*, 2:247.

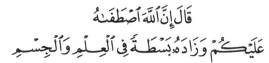

chroniclers and scribes. It reminds one of other false attributions made regarding certain chosen prophets and messengers of God. These include adultery and murder attributed to David,[165] incest attributed to Lot,[166] and the making of idols and/or their worship ascribed to Aaron[167] and Solomon![168] Such evidence clearly indicates that the Bible narratives have been altered and thus cannot be accepted as truth. Furthermore, it is obvious that the story of Saul's seeking and requesting a conjuress to call up the soul of the deceased Samuel is nothing but a figment of the Jewish chroniclers' imaginations. They have woven this myth into the story of the noble King Saul's life in order to discredit him as a leader of Israel. The Israelites were never pleased with his appointment over them, even though it was by divine will, as mentioned in the Qur'ān.[169] They objected to his appointment to authority over them for he was from the tribe of Benjamin, the smallest tribe in Israel; he had neither wealth nor position in the Israelite society.[170] They unwillingly accepted Saul as king only after they were shown a miraculous sign of his authority -the lost Ark of the Covenant[171] being brought back to them, carried by

---

165 See II Samuel, 11:2-5.

166 See Genesis, 19:30-38.

167 See Exodus, 32:1-6.

168 See I Kings, 11:1-10.

169 See Sūrah *al-Baqarah*, 2:247.

170 See al-Qurṭubi's monumental *tafsīr*, *al-Jāmiʿ u li Aḥkām al-Qur'ān*, vol. 3, p. 246.

171 According to Exodus 25:10-22, the Ark of the Covenant (*Tābūt*) was a chest of acacia wood covered and lined with pure gold. It contained the "testimony of God" (i.e., The Ten Commandments) and other relics. During the wars with the Philistines, Israel was severely defeated with great slaughter. Instead of relying upon their faith and being patient and courageous, they brought out the Ark of the Covenant as if it would help them in the fight. The enemy captured it, carried it away and later abandoned it in some village where it lay hidden for years. See I Samuel, 6-7.

angels. It contained assurances from their Lord and relics left by the family of Moses and Aaron.[172]

There are some narrations in historical works[173] which would appear to affirm Samuel's rising from his grave to rebuke Saul, however, these are weak narrations and cannot be accepted as evidence.[174] Ibn Kathīr relates the narration of al-Suddī and then says, "In this story there is much to doubt, and some parts of it are definitely rejectable." He also mentions another narration of al-Thaʿlabī in which it is related that Saul was directed to the grave of Samuel, who rose from the dead and began rebuking him for what he had done after the latter's passing. Ibn Kathīr follows this with a critical comment, saying that it is possible that Saul saw Samuel (in a vision) during sleep, not that Samuel actually rose alive from his grave. For that could not happen except as a miracle given to a prophet or messenger of God, and neither Saul nor the woman with him fulfill this necessary criterion.[175]

The final scripture of the revealed word of Allāh, the Qur'ān, was disclosed in order to affirm what is true of previous scriptures, to correct errors and false concepts in them, and to act as both a guard over the divine message and a test as to its correct interpretation. Allāh states in the Qur'ān:

وَأَنزَلْنَآ إِلَيْكَ ٱلْكِتَٰبَ
بِٱلْحَقِّ مُصَدِّقًا لِّمَا بَيْنَ يَدَيْهِ مِنَ ٱلْكِتَٰبِ وَمُهَيْمِنًا
عَلَيْهِ ۖ فَٱحْكُم بَيْنَهُم بِمَآ أَنزَلَ ٱللَّهُ ۖ وَلَا تَتَّبِعْ أَهْوَآءَهُمْ
عَمَّا جَآءَكَ مِنَ ٱلْحَقِّ

---

[172] See Sūrah *al-Baqarah*, 2:247.

[173] See, for example, lbn Kathīr's *al-Bidāyah wan- Nihāyah*, vol. 2, p. 9 and Ibn *al-Athīr's al-Kāmil fit-Tārīkh*, vol. 1, p. 22.

[174] These narrations are termed "*isrā'īliyyāt*" (Jewish traditions) and are therefore rejected.

[175] See Ibn Kathīr's *al-Bidāyah wan- Nihāyah*, vol. 2, p. 9.

> "And We have revealed to you, [O Muḥammad], the scripture in truth, confirming the scripture which preceded it and guarding over it. So judge between them by what Allāh has revealed, and do not follow their vain desires, thus diverging from the truth which has come to you."[176]

This verse clearly specifies that the Qur'ān confirms only that which is the unaltered truth of the previous scriptures and guards this recurring message from Allāh. The criteria for judging truth in scripture are the Qur'ān and the sunnah,[177] for they correct errors and distortions which have crept into the divinely revealed books prior to the Qur'ān.

Alleged Evidence from the Qur'ān and its Refutation

Ṭanṭāwī Jawharī uses various verses from Sūrah *al-Baqarah* as "proof" that souls of the dead return and converse with people who are awake and that there exists the possibility of conjuring the dead. Although each of the following verses are examples of Allāh's infinite power epitomized by His ability to bring the dead back to life, the subject of these verses falls outside the realm of dispute, and thus the verses carry no weight in support of his claim. Therefore, it is essential to examine each set of verses in order to refute Jawharī's viewpoint.

وَإِذْ
قَتَلْتُمْ نَفْسًا فَادَّارَأْتُمْ فِيهَا ۖ وَاللَّهُ مُخْرِجٌ مَا كُنْتُمْ تَكْتُمُونَ ﴿٧٢﴾
فَقُلْنَا اضْرِبُوهُ بِبَعْضِهَا ۚ كَذَٰلِكَ يُحْيِي اللَّهُ الْمَوْتَىٰ وَيُرِيكُمْ
آيَاتِهِ لَعَلَّكُمْ تَعْقِلُونَ ﴿٧٣﴾

---

176 Sūrah *al-Mā'idah*, 5:48.

177 The sunnah is also a form of revelation except that it differs from the Qur'ān in its form of delivery to the Prophet (ﷺ), and it is no less binding than the Qur'ān. In fact, a reference to the sunnah along with the Qur'ān is mandatory. For details, see al-Albānī's treatise, *Manzilat al-Sunnati fil-Islām*.

"Remember when you slew a man and accused each other regarding it? But Allāh was to bring forth that which you were hiding. So We said, 'Strike him with a part of it [i. e., the heifer].' Thus Allāh brings the dead to life and shows you His signs[178] so that you may understand."[179]

أَوْ كَٱلَّذِى مَرَّ
عَلَىٰ قَرْيَةٍ وَهِىَ خَاوِيَةٌ عَلَىٰ عُرُوشِهَا قَالَ أَنَّىٰ يُحْىِۦ هَٰذِهِ ٱللَّهُ
بَعْدَ مَوْتِهَا ۖ فَأَمَاتَهُ ٱللَّهُ مِا۟ئَةَ عَامٍ ثُمَّ بَعَثَهُۥ ۖ قَالَ كَمْ لَبِثْتَ ۖ
قَالَ لَبِثْتُ يَوْمًا أَوْ بَعْضَ يَوْمٍ ۖ قَالَ بَل لَّبِثْتَ مِا۟ئَةَ عَامٍ
فَٱنظُرْ إِلَىٰ طَعَامِكَ وَشَرَابِكَ لَمْ يَتَسَنَّهْ ۖ وَٱنظُرْ إِلَىٰ
حِمَارِكَ وَلِنَجْعَلَكَ ءَايَةً لِّلنَّاسِ ۖ وَٱنظُرْ إِلَى
ٱلْعِظَامِ كَيْفَ نُنشِزُهَا ثُمَّ نَكْسُوهَا لَحْمًا ۚ فَلَمَّا
تَبَيَّنَ لَهُۥ قَالَ أَعْلَمُ أَنَّ ٱللَّهَ عَلَىٰ كُلِّ شَىْءٍ قَدِيرٌ ﴿٢٥٩﴾

"Or take the similitude of one who, passing by the ruins of a village, exclaimed, 'How will Allāh give this [place] life after its death?' So Allāh caused him to die for one hundred years and then brought him back to life. He said, 'How long have you remained?'[180] [The man] replied, 'I remained a day or a portion of a day.' He rejoined, 'No, but you have remained for one hundred years. Just look at your food and drink which have not changed with time! And look at your donkey! And We will make you a sign unto the people. And look at the bones - how We bring them together and clothe them with

---

[178] His miraculous, wondrous powers which have no limit.

[179] Sūrah *al-Baqarah*, 2:72-73.

[180] Allāh conveyed to him this question as a voice from the sky or by sending Jibrīl to him with the question. See al-Qurṭubī's *al-Jāmiʿ u li Aḥkām al-Qur'ān*, vol. 3, p. 291.

flesh.' When the matter became clear to him, he said, 'Verily, I know that Allāh has power over all things.'"[181]

وَإِذْ قَالَ إِبْرَٰهِـۧمُ رَبِّ أَرِنِى كَيْفَ تُحْىِ ٱلْمَوْتَىٰ ۖ قَالَ أَوَلَمْ
تُؤْمِن ۖ قَالَ بَلَىٰ وَلَـٰكِن لِّيَطْمَئِنَّ قَلْبِى ۖ قَالَ فَخُذْ أَرْبَعَةً مِّنَ
ٱلطَّيْرِ فَصُرْهُنَّ إِلَيْكَ ثُمَّ ٱجْعَلْ عَلَىٰ كُلِّ جَبَلٍ مِّنْهُنَّ جُزْءًا
ثُمَّ ٱدْعُهُنَّ يَأْتِينَكَ سَعْيًا ۚ وَٱعْلَمْ أَنَّ ٱللَّهَ عَزِيزٌ حَكِيمٌ ﴿٢٦٠﴾

"And when Ibrāhīm said, 'My Lord, show me how You give life to the dead,' [Allāh] said, 'Do you not believe?' [Ibrāhīm] replied, 'Surely I do, but [I ask] only so that my heart be satisfied.' [Allāh] said, 'Take four birds and bring them to you. Then place a portion of them upon every hill and call to them. They will come [flying] to you in haste.[182] And know that Allāh is Mighty, Wise.'"[183]

The first set of verses deals with the story of Mūsā (Moses) and the Children of Israel, regarding an incident of murder which occurred among them. Mūsā had been given divine orders to direct the people to slaughter a heifer, which they finally did after much procrastination. They were ordered to take some portion of the heifer's flesh and to strike the body of the murdered person in order that Allāh might bring him back to life momentarily, thereby revealing his killer. Allāh gives a parable of His infinite powers by this wondrous miracle at the hands of His chosen messenger, Mūsā. Allāh brought the slain man to life momentarily not only to reveal the killer but also as a means of impressing upon the minds

---

[181] Sūrah *al-Baqarah,* 2:259.

[182] That is, all of the cut-up portions will unite once again to form the live birds from which they were cut. They will then fly back to Ibrāhīm alive and sound. So, too, will human bodies be revived and joined with their souls and then come "flying" to their Lord.

[183] Sūrah *al-Baqarah,* 2:260.

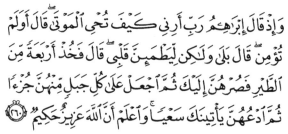

of the Children of Israel (and all of mankind) that He is capable of instantly resurrecting all men from their graves for the Final Judgement.[184] In a similar way, the second set of verses relates the manner in which Allāh revived another person[185] to life after one hundred years. Like the first set of verses, this merely reiterates the well-known fact that Allāh, the Exalted and Mighty, performs wondrous miracles through His prophets. And finally, the third set of verses illustrates how Allāh brought the dismembered parts of four birds together and back to life - another example of His omnipotence and ability to reunite the human body with its soul.

Such miracles by Allāh, the Blessed and Exalted, are numerous[186] but in no way carry weight as evidence for what has been alleged by Jawharī, namely, that the souls of the dead are able to come to the living (who are awake) on the earth, meet and converse with them, etc. What has been established in these sets of verses is that such miracles were special circumstances of the chosen messengers of Allāh. However, with the finality of prophethood - which culminated in the mission of the seal of all prophets and messengers, Muḥammad (ﷺ) - such miracles no longer occur.

Alleged Evidence from Observable Phenomena and its Refutation

The final piece of "evidence" put forward by Ṭanṭāwī Jawharī regarding this issue is certain "observable" phenomena which he

184 See Ibn Kathīr's *Tafsīr al-Qur'ān al-ʿAẓīm*, vol. 1, p. 201.

185 The exact identity of this person is not known, and is actually of little relevance. The important fact is that Allāh made him a sign for others, establishing for them beyond a doubt that He is capable of bringing the dead back to life for the Judgement. For details, see al-Ālūsī's *Rūḥ al-Maʿānī*, vol. 3, p. 20 and al-Qurṭubī's *al-Jāmiʿ*, vol. 3, p. 289.

186 The aforementioned are examples of Allāh Himself reviving different forms of creation, however, His miracles are not confined to only this means of resurrection. For example, Allāh enabled one of His chosen messengers, Prophet Jesus, to give life to the dead by His permission. For details, see Sūrah *al-Mā'idah,* 5:110.

documents at length in his *tafsīr*.[187] In order to expose the real nature and essence of these strange experiences and circumstances, it is necessary to mention some examples of such phenomena.

It is reported that strange sounds, noises and/or "voices" have been heard emanating from deserted houses and buildings, as well as occupied dwellings. It is said that strange knocking or tapping sounds were heard by the occupants. Sometimes the sounds resembled the eerie wailing of wind in a violent storm. At other times they resembled the monotonous sounds of machinery or violent thunder and canon shots. On some occasions objects in the house and even the house itself were affected by such phenomena. They trembled, shook and convulsed upon such occurrences. It has been further observed on occasion that voices resembling humans issued from certain parts of the house. The sound of musical instruments playing in unison or singly were heard, but no player was found or instruments seen![188]

Other strange phenomena reported by eyewitnesses include the visions of strange lights which glow in different shapes and colours in darkened rooms which are void of electric, chemical or phosphorescent sources. Furthermore, thousands of people have witnessed certain hidden forces acting on heavy material objects, sometimes lifting them and at other times turning them over or carrying them away. Such circumstances as previously mentioned contradict natural forces and are beyond human comprehension.[189] Even stranger than this is the appearance of certain "spirits" (claimed to be the souls of the dead returned to the earth) which convey "news" about certain future events[190] which turn out to be true! Certain thinkers, including Jawharī, believe

---

[187] See Vol. 1, pp. 84-89 and vol. 9, pp. 92-117.

[188] See *Tafsīr al-Jawāhir*, vol. 1, p. 87.

[189] Ibid., p. 86.

[190] Such as the death of a person, an accident, etc.

that such phenomena is explained by the return of the dead to the earth. However, these occurrences can be explained in an acceptable and satisfactory manner in complete consonance with the divine revelation of Islām as exemplified in the Qur'ān and the sunnah. In light of these sources, it can confidently be said that such phenomena is the work of beings termed "*jinn*"[191] (invisible creatures of extraordinary powers and capabilities). These creatures reside mainly in deserted buildings. Often times they take them over, and when humans move in, the *jinn* attempt to scare them off by creating mischief, eerie noises and displaying strange visual phenomena as well. This explains the popular stories of people's experiences with "haunted" houses and with so-called "spirits," "spooks" or "ghosts," which understood by many to be the souls of the dead returned to earth. In reality, these are evil *jinn* (devils), which can be evicted from homes by recitation of the *basmalah*[192] and by various portions of the Qur'ān, especially *Āyat al-kursī*[193] and Sūrah *al-Baqarah*.[194]

The lifting, lowering, turning or carrying of heavy material objects without any apparent source is due to the amazing superhuman powers of these beings as indicated in the Qur'ān, and the sunnah. In the famous Qur'ānic story of Prophet Sulaymān (Solomon), a *jinnī* offered to bring the queen of Sheba's throne

---

[191] The *jinn* are of two kinds - pious, useful believers and foul, evil disbelievers. The latter are termed "*Shayāṭīn*" (devils). For an excellent study of the nature and circumstances of these extraordinary creatures, see the treatise, *'Ālam al-Jinn wa al-Shayāṭīn* by 'Umar Sulaymān al-Ashqar.

[192] The formula: "*Bismillāh ar-Raḥmān ar-Raḥīm*" ("In the name of Allāh, the Entirely Merciful, the Especially Merciful").

[193] Sūrah *al-Baqarah*, 2:255. The effectiveness of this recitation is related in *Ṣaḥīḥ al-Bukhārī*.

[194] The effectiveness of this recitation is related in various authentic traditions. See also *'Ālam al-Jinn*, p. 23.

to Prophet Sulaymān by speeding from Jerusalem to Yemen and back in the twinkling of an eye.[195]

Visions of strange lights, forms and colours, etc. are actually the work of *jinn*, who are capable of taking on or producing many different forms and shapes. Ibn Taymiyyah relates that he was informed by a "*shaykh*"[196] who had connections with *jinn* that upon occasion they would show the latter a glimmering shape whose surface was like glass or water on which was displayed a visual "reply" to certain questions or news.[197]

The Conjuring of Souls and its Refutation

Ṭanṭāwī Jawharī dedicates a sizable segment of his *tafsīr*[198] to an exposition of how souls of the dead can be "called up" by those who are skilled, sincere and patient. He relates many cases (some of which he personally witnessed) where the apparition or "flesh-and-blood" form of a deceased person appeared before an audience of people. Sometimes the soul of the deceased was incarnated through a second party, a "medium," who served as the "vessel" for the dead person's soul. However, the voice and personality which emanated from the body of the medium was that of the dead person himself. This phenomenon is also the work of *jinn*,[199] usually in agreement and cooperation with the

---

[195] See Sūrah *al-Naml*, 27:39-40.

[196] Used here to mean a follower or mentor of one of the many Sūfic (mystical) paths invented by so-called Muslims as a way or method spiritual purification.

[197] Ibn Taymiyyah's *Majmū' al-Fatāwā*, vol. 11, p. 309. See also its abridged translation under the title "Ibn Taymīyah's Essay on the *Jinn*" by Abū Ameenah Bilal Philips.

[198] See vol. 9, pp. 92-117 for details.

[199] In reality, a *jinnī* occupies the medium's body and speaks with the dead person's "voice" and mannerisms. This has been observed by many dependable Islamic scholars, such as Ibn Taymiyyah. This is mentioned in his monumental treatise, *Majmū' al-Fatāwā* vol. 11, p. 665.

conjurer. Authentic traditions of the Prophet (ﷺ) state that the *jinn* are capable of taking on various shapes - human, animal or otherwise. For example, at the Battle of Badr a devil (evil *jinnī*) came to the polytheists of Quraysh in the shape of Surāqah bin Mālik and promised to stand in support of them. However, when the Muslims were aided by the descending angels, he turned on his heels and declared himself innocent of them.[200] Al-Bukhārī also relates the incident of the *jinnī* who came several times to Abū Hurayrah while he was in charge of the alms of *Ramaḍān*. The *jinnī* attempted to take from the foodstuffs being stored, and when apprehended by Abū Hurayrah, he excused himself by saying that he was extremely poor, that his family was in dire need, etc. Feeling sorry for him, Abū Hurayrah let him go but told the Prophet (ﷺ) about the incident. Allāh's Messenger (ﷺ) informed him that the "person" had lied to him and that he would return, which he did, attempting to steal the food again. When Abū Hurayrah seized him and threatened to bring him to the Prophet (ﷺ), the *jinnī* pleaded with Abū Hurayrah to let him go, promising to relate certain information which would benefit him. When asked what that was, he told Abū Hurayrah that the latter should read *Āyat al-Kursī* whenever he laid down on his bed to sleep. He explained that this would thereby protect him from evil, and no devil would come near him until he awakened the next morning. When Abū Hurayrah informed the Prophet (ﷺ) regarding what happened, the latter said to him, "He has told you the truth although he is a great liar; do you know who he was, Abū Hurayrah?" Abū Hurayrah replied, "No, I do not." The Prophet (ﷺ) rejoined, "That was a *shayṭān*."[201]

In addition to the aforementioned abilities, *jinn* can take the form of people who have died, as is recorded in detail by Ibn

---

[200] This incident is alluded to in the Qur'ān. See Sūrah *al-Anfāl*, 8:48. For details, see al-Qurṭubī's *al-Jāmiʿ*, vol. 8, pp. 26-27 and al-Ṭabarī's *Jāmiʿ al-Bayān* vol. 14, pp. 7-11.

[201] Related in *Ṣaḥīḥ al-Bukhārī*, vol. 6, p. 491, ḥadīth no. 530.

Taymiyyah.[202] He relates that *jinn* appear to misguided people who call upon certain deceased "saints" or other "pious" personalities;[203] they appear in the form of the peron who was petitioned and mislead the petitioner. Likewise, the *jinn* appear in the form of idols or enter one's idols, speaking to the idol worshippers.[204] This causes the people who witness such things to sink deeper into *shirk* (polytheistic attitudes, beliefs and practices), which is the greatest delight of evil *jinn*.[205]

The claim that these "spirits" (thought to be the dead returned to earth) foretell future events which indeed come to pass can be explained by revelation from the prophetic sunnah. The following text confirms that such phenomena are the work of *jinn*, not the souls of the dead themselves:

عن أبي هريرة أن النبي (ﷺ) قال: إذا قضى الله الأمر في السماء ضربت الملائكة بأجنحتها خضعانا لقوله كأنه سلسلة على صفوان ينفذهم ذلك. فإذا فزع عن قلوبهم قالوا: ماذا قال ربكم؟ قالوا: الذي قاله الحق، وهو العلي الكبير، فيسمعه مسترقو السمع هكذا، واحد فوق آخر، (ووصف سفيان بيده، وفرج بين أصابع يده اليمنى نصبها بعضها فوق بعض)، فربما أدرك الشهاب المستمع قبل أن يرمي بها إلى صاحبه فيحرقه، وربما

---

[202] See his *Majmū' al-Fatāwā*, vol. 1, pp. 157-159, 171-178, 359-365 and vol. 27, pp. 172-179.

[203] These misguided people call upon the dead for help of some kind or for an answer to their prayers.

[204] This occurs often. For example, some Christians claim that the "Virgin Mary" has appeared to certain Catholics in various eras. However, these appearances were, in fact, made by *jinn* in order to further mislead the disbelievers in their polytheism.

[205] See *Majmū' al-Fatāwā*, vol. 11, pp. 664-665.

لم يدركه حتى يرمي بها إلى الذي يليه، إلى الذي هو أسفل منه، حتى يلقوها إلى الأرض (وربما قال سفيان: حتى تنتهي إلى الأرض) فتلقى على فم الساحر [والكاهن] فيكذب معها مئة كذبة فيصدق، فيقولون: ألم يخبرنا يوم كذا وكذا بكذا وكذا، فوجدناه للتي سمعت من السماء

Abū Hurayrah reported that the Prophet (ﷺ) said: "When from the heavens Allāh ordains a thing[206] to be, the angels strike their wings in humility and submission to His command. [The noise resounds] like the ringing clatter of metal on a smooth stone and strikes terror into their very hearts. The angels ask the others [commissioned with the task], 'What did your Lord say?' They reply, 'He has said the truth, and He is the Sublime and Magnificent.' Then the eavesdroppers [i.e., *jinn*] pick up the news [of the ordained matter] from where they sit, one above the other. [One of the narrators, Sufyān, spread the fingers of his right hand slightly, one above the other, in order to describe it.] Sometimes[207] a shooting star strikes a listener [i.e., a *jinnī*] before he can pass the ordained matter down to his companion below him, thereby burning him to extinction. Occasionally, the shooting star does not reach the *jinnī* until he has passed the information to the other *jinnī* under him, and thereafter to the one below him, and so on until it reaches the earth. It then falls upon the tongue of a magician or soothsayer who then adds to it one hundred lies,[208] which are believed. Thus people say, 'Did he not inform us on such and such a day regarding such and such a matter and now we find it exactly

---

[206] Such as death, disaster, good fortune, rain, drought, etc.

[207] "Most of the time," according to other narrations, for it is rare indeed that the *jinn* escape being destroyed by the shooting, celestial fire. See *Fatḥ al-Bāri*, vol. 8, p. 539.

[208] That is, he adds to this true piece of news a myriad of falsehoods.

so?'[209] They say this in reference to that which was heard from the heavens."[210]

According to this ḥadīth, such occasions of future events are sometimes "pirated" by *jinn* and sometimes conveyed to magicians, soothsayers and fortunetellers. No doubt, these same *jinn* who appear in the "person" of the deceased or who occupy the body of a medium occasionally "foretell" - through this means - a future event which, in fact, comes to pass. In reality, they do not "foretell" or prophesy but merely pass on a piece of "pirated" information gleaned from "news" of the heavens. The *jinn*, pretending to be the souls of the dead returned to the earth, occasionally give a rare piece of information to those likely to believe in the return of the dead, thereby causing them to become attached to and dependent upon them. This leads such misguided people further into *shirk*. This is quite obvious historically[211] and is apparent in modern secret societies for the worship of the dead and Satan, and the revival of witchcraft and sorcery.[212]

Jinn are capable of appearing in strange forms of all sorts. It is related in authentic traditions[213] that they may take the form

---

[209] Although a soothsayer may correctly predict a future event, along with this one bit of truth which has been passed on to him by the *jinn*, he adds scores of lies in order to keep people under his influence for material and social gains.

[210] Related in *Ṣaḥīḥ al-Bukhārī*, vol. 8, p. 150, , ḥadīth no. 232.

[211] Many ancient people of the East and certain tribes of the North-American Indians had certain beliefs and rituals connected with the conjuring up and worship of the dead, especially their respected family members.

[212] Such secret societies are numerous in the West, especially in Britain and the United States, as well as in the rest of Europe and Canada, to a lesser extent.

[213] See *Ṣaḥīḥ al-Bukhārī*, vol. 1, p. 290, , ḥadīth no. 488 and *Ṣaḥīḥ Muslim*, vol. 1, pp. 261-262, ḥadīth no. 1032 and vol. 4, pp. 1211-1212, ḥadīth numbers 5542-5545.

of certain animals, such as camels, donkeys, cats, dogs, snakes, etc.[214] Therefore, it is no surprise that *jinn* are able to assume the form of a deceased person, thereby giving the impression that the souls of the dead return to the earth. However, it has been clearly established through illustrations from the texts of divine revelation that, in reality, the return of such souls to the earth does not occur. Rather, it is made to appear so. It is done in order to confuse people and to lead them astray from the path of *tawḥīd* (pure unity of the worship of the One and Only Almighty God, Allāh) to the path of *shirk* (the association of others with Allāh in all or part of that which is the sole realm and right of Allāh). This is the ultimate mission of disbelieving *jinn*. Causing people to believe in the return of souls is one of the means adopted by *Iblīs* and his army of evil *jinn* to misguide mankind. By pretending to be "returned" souls of the dead along with the performance of extraordinary superhuman feats, they dupe people into believing in the "powers" of the dead. The cult of "conjuring" souls has become a religious science of its own. Ultimately, it leads to the worship of the souls of the dead[215] and, in reality, the worship of Satan himself.

In conclusion, it is abundantly clear that souls of the dead cannot and do not come back to the earth in transmigration nor in any other form or shape. Furthermore, they cannot appear to or converse with the living (who are awake) inhabitants of the earth. Rather, such phenomena, which appear to point to such a belief, have been proven to be the work of evil *jinn* whose purpose is to misguide mankind from the path of truth to the path of falsehood. Praise be to Almighty Allāh, who has made all things clear by way of His protected divine revelation.

---

214 For details along with examples, see *ʿĀlam al-Jinn wa al-Shayāṭīn*, p.29.

215 See Ibn Taymiyyah's *Majmūʿ al-Fatāwā*, vol. 1, pp. 359-361.

The Soul's Abode Between Death and the Resurrection

The scholars of Islām, even the theologians of *ahl al-sunnah*, differed widely on the issue of the soul's abode between death and the Resurrection. The existence of vast numbers of narrations relating to this subject is the main reason for such differences. These traditions are of varying degrees of authenticity, and many of them are weak or forged. Therefore, in order to ensure that only the authentic narrations are applied and to arrive at the correct view on this issue, a careful, critical sifting of the pertinent ḥadīth literature in this area is absolutely essential. Furthermore, a synthesis of the various textual material from both the Qur'ān and the authentic sunnah must be completed in order to arrive at a comprehensive, all encompassing view of the matter. Such a method will remove the seeming confusion due to apparently conflicting reports. The various views regarding this question will be analyzed along with the proof used to support them, and finally, preference will be given to the view which is supported by the most authentic texts and sound reasoning.

Various Opinions[216]

1. Generally, it is said that the souls of the believers are in Paradise whether they be martyrs or not. However, they may

[216] See Ibn al-Qayyim's *Kitāb al-Rūḥ*, pp. 133-134 and *Lawāmiʿ al-Anwār*, vol. 2, pp. 46-47.

be temporarily prevented from entering it due to major sins or an outstanding debt - unless Allāh accepts them with mercy and forgiveness. This view was held by the two illustrious companions, Abū Hurayrah and ʿAbdullāh bin ʿUmar, among others.

2. As related by his son ʿAbdullāh, Imām Aḥmad claimed that the souls of the disbelievers are in the Fire, while the souls of the believers are in Paradise.

3. Similar to the previous one, another view states that the believers' souls are in *ʿilliyyūn* (the paradisal heights of the seventh heaven), while the souls of the disbelievers are in *sijjīn* (the seventh earth) below the armies of *Iblīs*.

4. A group of the companions and their followers (*tābiʿūn*) held that the believers' souls are with Allāh and left it at that.

5. Another group of scholars maintained that the souls of the believers are at the door of Paradise, and there comes to them its fragrant breezes, bounties and pleasures. But according to Mujāhid, only the soul of the martyr is at the door of Paradise.

6. Imām Mālik stated, "It has reached me that the *rūḥ* is free to roam wherever it wants."

7. Another group of scholars claimed that the souls of the dead are in the expanses of their graves.

8. Yet another view, which partially resembles numbers three and seven, stated, "The believers' souls are in a "*barzakh*" (zone) of the earth, moving about as they please, whereas the souls of the disbelievers are in *sijjīn*.

9. A different view claimed that the souls of the believers are on the right-hand side of Ādam, while the souls of the disbelievers are on his left.

10. Others held that the souls of the believers are at al-Jābiyah,[217] while the souls of the disbelievers are at a place called Burhūt[218] in Ḥadhramawt.

11. The last view is similar to the preceding one except that it claimed that the believers' souls are at the well of Zamzam,[219] while the disbelievers' souls are at the dried well of Burhūt.

Analysis and Assessment of the Different Views

Views numbers ten and eleven must be rejected outright because they are not supported by authentic traditions. Rather, all the ḥadīths or *āthār* (narrations traced back to the companions or their followers) used to support these views are weak (*ḍaʿīf*) and rejected (*munkar*).[220] Furthermore, these views contradict the Qur' an and the authentic texts of the sunnah, as shall be established later on.

Similar is the case of the view stated in number nine. Although it is based on the authentic tradition regarding *al-Isrā'* (The Night Journey of Prophet Muḥammad (ﷺ)), it is not acceptable for a number of reasons. Firstly, the narration of the Prophet's vision of Ādam in Paradise on the night of his journey and ascension has been misinterpreted. The Prophet (ﷺ) related:

فإذا رجل قاعد على يمينه أسودة وعلى يساره أسودة، إذا نظر قبل يمينه ضحك وإذا نظر قبل يساره بكى. قلت لجبريل: من هذا ؟ قال: هذا آدم، وهذه الأسودة عن يمينه وشماله نسم بنيه، فأهل اليمين منهم أهل الجنة والأسودة التي عن شماله أهل النار

[217] Literally, a basin or pool in which water collects.

[218] A dry, salty piece of land in an arid valley of Yemen on which almost nothing grows.

[219] The well situated below the floor of the Sacred Mosque in Makkah which produces blessed water.

[220] For details, see footnotes to pp. 153-154 of *Kitāb al-Rūḥ*.

"And there was a man seated with a crowd of people on his right and others on his left. When he looked to his right he laughed, and when he looked to his left he wept. I said to Jibrīl, 'Who is this?' He replied, 'This is Ādam, and the crowd on his right and left are the number of his offspring. Those on the right are the people of Paradise, while those on his left are the people of the Fire.'"[221]

Some scholars understood this tradition in a literal sense - that the souls of the deceased offspring of Ādam are presently in Heaven on his right and left. However, the correct understanding of this ḥadīth is that the souls of the deceased are not actually on the right and left-hand sides of Ādam. Rather, this ḥadīth indicates that an illustration was depicted for the Prophet (ﷺ) to allow him to visualize the respective conditions of mankind, in general, and of his *ummah*, in particular. Secondly, if this ḥadīth is interpreted literally, it contradicts a number of Qur'amc verses and other prophetic traditions which clearly stipulate that the souls of the disbelievers are not in Paradise. A sample of these will follow later. In conclusion, like the two preceding ones, this view is untenable because it contradicts the Qur'ān and the sunnah.

Having dispensed with those views which are totally unacceptable, the remaining ones will be discussed. It is important to clarify at the outset that all of these views (numbers 1-8) have a certain truth in them but are marred by clear shortcomings in that they convey only a partial view of the available, comprehensive picture regarding this subject.

The most correct opinion regarding the souls abode between death and the Resurrection is that human souls in the *barzakh* are of two kinds: those of the believers and those of the disbelievers. However, there is a great deal of difference in the degrees and circumstances of those belonging to either of these two categories. For example, the souls of Allāh's chosen prophets and messengers

---

[221] Authentically related by Muslim, et. al.

are in the highest of the heavenly heights (*ʿilliyyūn*). And even their abodes differ, as is apparent from the authentic traditions[222] about Prophet Muḥammad's Night Journey (*Isrā'*) and Ascension (*Miʿrāj*) into the heavens, where he was shown some of Allāh's signs.[223] The souls of other deceased believers are also in Paradise but are only enjoying some of its pleasures in a restricted measure according to their degrees with Allāh.

Regarding martyrs, there is the following tradition:

عن ابن عباس قال: قال رسول الله (ﷺ): لما أصيب إخوانكم - يعني يوم أحد - جعل الله أرواحهم في أجواف طير خضر ترد أنهار الجنة وتأكل من ثمارها وتأوي إلى قناديل من ذهب مدلاة في ظل العرش. فلما وجدوا طيب مأكلهم ومشربهم ومقيلهم، قالوا: من يبلغ إخواننا أنا أحياء في الجنة نرزق، لئلا ينكلوا عن الحرب ولايزهدوا في الجهاد؟ قال: فقال عز وجل: أنا أبلغهم عنكم، فأنزل الله تعالى: ﴿وَلاَ تَحْسَبَنَّ الَّذِينَ قُتِلُواْ فِي سَبِيلِ اللّهِ أَمْوَاتًا بَلْ أَحْيَاء عِندَ رَبِّهِمْ يُرْزَقُونَ﴾

Ibn ʿAbbās reported that Allāh's Messenger (ﷺ) said. "When your brethren were killed [on the Day of *Uḥud*],[224] Allāh placed their souls inside the bodies of green birds which come to the rivers of Paradise, partake of its fruits, and then retire to golden lamps hanging from the shade of the Throne. When they taste the goodness of their food, drink and shelter, they cry, 'Who will inform our brethren that we are alive and are provided sustenance in Paradise so that they may not desist

[222] Related by al-Bukhari, Muslim, et. al.

[223] For a detailed exposition of the Night Journey and Ascension, see Ibn Kathīr's *Tafsīr al-Qur'ān al-ʿAẓīm*, vol. 5, pp. 3-42.

[224] What is in brackets is the explanation of the narrator. By the "Day of *Uḥud*" is meant the Battle of *Uḥud*, even though it took more than one day.

from fighting and not abstain from *jihād*?' So Allāh, the Almighty and Majestic, said, 'I will inform them about you.' Then Allāh, the Exalted, revealed [the Qur'ānic verse]: 'Do not consider those who are slain in the path of Allāh as dead. Rather, they are alive with their Lord, being provided for.'"[225]

In explanation of this ḥadīth, Ibn al-Qayyim commented that Allāh places the souls of martyrs inside the bodies of green birds. For having sacrificed themselves solely for His cause until His enemies destroyed them, Allāh replaces their bodies with forms better than their earthly ones. The pleasure of these martyrs is achieved by means of such forms, in a more complete manner than could be achieved by the soul alone.[226] Even so, such a pleasure is only a faint foretaste of what is in store for the martyr when he attains his full state of pleasure on the Day of Judgement.[227]

The souls of other pious believers are also in Paradise, as is clear from the following tradition:

عن كعب بن مالك أن رسول الله (ﷺ) قال: إنما نسمة المؤمن طير يعلق في شجر الجنة حتى يرجعه الله إلى جسده يوم يبعثه

Ka'b bin Mālik related that Allāh's Messenger (ﷺ) said. "The believer's soul is [like] a bird which feeds upon fruits of the trees of Paradise until Allāh returns it to its body on the day he is resurrected."[228]

Some scholars[229] claimed that in this tradition the phrase "the believer's soul" indicates only the martyr's soul, insinuating that they are the only ones (other than Allāh's chosen prophets and

---

[225] Related by Aḥmad and al-Ḥākim with *ḥasan sanad*. The Qur'ānic reference is Sūrah *Āl 'Imrān,* 3:169.

[226] See *Kitāb al-Rūḥ*, p. 143.

[227] Ibid., p. 142.

[228] Authentically related by Mālik, Aḥmad, et. al.

[229] Such as al-Qurṭubī, Ibn al-'Arabī, lbn 'Abdul-Barr, among others.

messengers) who go directly to Paradise and taste of its fruits. However, this view is untenable for the text of this ḥadīth mentions clearly the believer's soul without restricting it to that of the martyr.[230] Synthesizing all of the various narrations on this subject brings one to the conclusion that there is a clear difference between the descriptions of a martyr's soul and those of a common, pious believer's soul. The martyr's soul is within the body of a green bird, whereas the common believer's soul is like a bird, feeding from the fruits of Paradise.[231] As has been mentioned, the form in which a martyr's soul abides facilitates a more pleasurable experience of Paradise than the form in which the common believer's soul exists.

Regarding these martyrs and common believers, certain additional circumstances further restrict their conditions. For example, if the martyr or believer has a debt, his soul is temporarily restricted from the state of pleasure previously described. This is illustrated in the following two traditions:

عن محمد بن عبد الله بن جحش أن رجلا جاء إلى النبي (ﷺ) فقال: يا رسول الله مالي إن قتلت في سبيل الله؟ قال: الجنة. فلما ولى قال: إلا الدين سارني به جبريل آنفا

> Muḥammad bin ʿAbdullāh bin Jaḥsh reported: "A man came to the Prophet (ﷺ), saying, 'O Messenger of Allāh, what would be in store for me if I were slain in the path of Allāh?' He (ﷺ) replied, 'Paradise.' The man turned and began to walk away, whereupon Allāh's Messenger (ﷺ) called out to

---

230 For a detailed explanation of this point, see al-Kandahlāwī's *Awjaz al-Masālik ilā Muwaṭṭa' Mālik*, vol. 4, pp. 295-298.

231 See *Kitāb al-Rūḥ*, p. 144. It is said that this is because the martyr's soul is transported by the green bird, whereas the other souls have to move on their own. (ed.)

him, 'Unless you have a debt.[232] Jibrīl just informed me of this.'"[233]

عن أبي هريرة قال: قال رسول الله (ﷺ): نفس المؤمن معلقة بدينه حتى يقضى عنه

Abū Hurayrah related that Allāh's Messenger (ﷺ) said: "The believer's soul is kept in suspension by [reason of] his debt until it is paid for him."[234]

The first tradition refers specifically to the case of the martyr slain in the path of Allāh, while the second is more general in scope, encompassing all other believers. They both convey the fact that the soul is suspended and prevented from entering Paradise due to debts.

In addition to the soul of a martyr or a pious, common believer, the soul of an impious believer may also be prevented from directly entering Paradise as a result of major sins. Examples of such cases have been mentioned in detail in the authentic sunnah, especially in the traditions of the Prophet's *Isrā'* and *Mi'rāj*,[235] in which he was shown visions of various punishments of the *barzakh* undergone by the sinful believers of the Islāmic *ummah*. The following is a small sample of such traditions:

عن أنس بن مالك قال: قال رسول الله (ﷺ): لما عرج بي مررت بقوم لهم أظفار من نحاس يخمشون وجوههم وصدورهم،

---

[232] If one had a debt, his soul would not enter Paradise immediately but would be temporarily forbidden entry until the debt was paid.

[233] Authentically related by Aḥmad.

[234] Authentically related by Aḥmad, al-Ḥākim, et. al.

[235] For a detailed commentary of these traditions, see Ibn al-Athīr's compilation entitled *Jāmi' al-Uṣūl*, vol. 2, pp. 530-535; the edition edited by 'Abdul-Qādir al-Arnā'ūṭ.

فقلت: يا جبريل من هؤلاء؟ قال: الذين يأكلون لحوم الناس ويقعون في أعراضهم

Anas bin Mālik reported that Allāh's Messenger (ﷺ) said.- "When I was taken up [during the Mi'rāj], I passed by some people with long copper fingernails with which they were tearing at their faces and chests. I said, 'O Jibrīl, who are those people?' He replied, 'They are those who eat peoples' flesh by defaming their honour and reputation.' "[236]

عن ابن عباس أن النبي (ﷺ) مر بقبرين فقال: إنهما ليعذبان، وما يعذبان في كبير، أما أحدهما فكان لا يستبرئ من البول وأما الآخر، فكان يمشي بالنميمة

Ibn 'Abbās related that the Prophet (ﷺ) passed by the graves of two men, whereupon he commented: "Verily, they are being punished but not for something major; one of them was not careful to remove all traces of urine,[237] while the other used to carry tales [i.e., hearsay] about others."[238]

Other traditions[239] describe the torment of the grave caused by some of the major sins which the Prophet (ﷺ) was shown during his ascension. For example, the liar was shown to be holding a hooked bar with which he tore one side of his mouth up to the nape of his neck. When that side returned to normal, he tore the other and so on, endlessly until the Day of Resurrection. Adulterers and adulteresses were seen naked in a pit resembling an oven with a wide

---

[236] Authentically related by Aḥmad and Abū Dāwūd. They "eat peoples' flesh" by slandering them or revealing to others their shortcomings, errors, etc. in order to purposely blacken their reputations.

[237] This includes making sure that the last drops are out and wiping it from the body so that nothing remains on one's clothing.

[238] Authentically related by al-Bukhārī and Muslim.

[239] For a major collection of these traditions, refer to Ibn Kathīr's *Tafsīr al-Qur'ān al-'Aẓīm*, vol. 5, pp. 3-42.

bottom and a narrow top. Fire blazed under them, and there was no escape from the narrow hole. The usurer was in a river of blood; and whenever he attempted to climb out, a large stone was thrown into his mouth, sending him back. These punishments will continue to be inflicted on such sinful people until the Hour is established.[240]

As previously mentioned (in view number five), there exists the opinion that the souls of all of the believers are at the door of Paradise and that its breezes and bounties come to them. However, *Mujāhid* maintained that it was only the souls of the martyrs which are at the door of Paradise. Perhaps they based their view on the following tradition:

عن ابن عباس قال: قال رسول الله (ﷺ): الشهداء على بارق نهر بباب الجنة في قبة خضراء، يخرج عليهم رزقهم من الجنة بكرة وعشية

Ibn ʿAbbās reported that Allāh's Messenger (ﷺ) said: "Martyrs are over a glistening river at the door of Paradise under a green dome. Their sustenance is brought to them from Paradise morning and evening."[241]

This text is not a valid proof for either of the two positions mentioned in view number five for several reasons. Firstly, clearer and stronger[242] texts have preceded which established beyond a doubt that, subject to certain conditions or prerequisites, the souls of believers are in Paradise. Secondly, this ḥadīth refers only to martyrs, not believers in general. Therefore, it cannot be used to

---

240 Abridged from narrations of al-Bukhārī and Muslim.

241 Related by Aḥmad, al-Ḥākim, al-Ṭabarānī, et. al. with a *ḥasan sanad*.

242 The previous ḥadīths regarding the believers, in general, and the martyrs, in particular, are "clearer" in that they are unambiguous and do not lend themselves to any interpretation other than the obvious meaning, whereas this tradition is open to interpretation. Moreover, the previous traditions are "stronger" because they were related in the most authentic compilations.

support the first position of view number five because it is incorrect to give a wider meaning to a tradition which is specific and limited in scope. And finally, the ḥadīth under discussion is open to many interpretations. It is possible that the river is at the door of Paradise and pours its sustenance and bounties upon the bodies of the martyrs which are in their graves (since it is maintained by a majority of scholars that the bodies of martyrs do not deteriorate but remain in a state as if alive). It is also possible that this ḥadīth refers to only a special category of martyrs who, for some reason or another,[243] are restricted from the full freedom of movement and pleasure afforded to their regular counterparts. However, just because this ḥadīth does not mention other categories of martyrs or other pious believers, it does not mean that they are not mentioned in other narrations. In any case, it can be justifiably argued that there is no real contradiction between this and previous traditions concerning the state of the martyr in Paradise. In fact, being at the door of Paradise does not necessarily mean outside its gates, as some like *Mujāhid* have supposed. Rather, it is more reasonable to assume that this latter narration merely describes one aspect of how martyrs are bestowed with various bounties of Paradise.

The claim that the souls of the dead are in the expanses of their graves (view number seven) applies to only certain people and under certain circumstances. It is correct to say that the soul of the disbeliever is confined to the punishment of the grave. Similarly, the soul of the impious believer is also confined to its grave and suffers torment for its sins for an appointed time until it is purified. However, if it was the soul of a truly foul and sinful Muslim (but one who did not deny the unity of Godhood and the prophethood of Muḥammad (ﷺ)), it could be confined in punishment until the Resurrection.[244] Additionally, although the soul of the pious

---

[243] Such as an outstanding debt or a lower degree of martyrdom.

[244] And even thereafter it could be relegated to the Hellfire for a very long appointed term, as has been related in the compilation of Muslim.

believer is in Paradise, it has the capability of returning to the grave in an instant[245] and in this state is shown its final resting place in Paradise.[246] Thus, it is only the disbelieving and/or the sinful believing souls which are completely confined to and imprisoned in their earthly graves, a befitting abode commensurate with their lowly and foul deeds while they were alive.

In light of the aforementioned information concerning the confinement of the disbelieving and/or the sinful believing souls to their graves, Imām Mālik's viewpoint (view number six), indicating that the *rūḥ* is free to roam about, applies only in the case of the pious believer.

The view expressed in number eight suggesting that the believers' souls are in a so-called "*barzakh*" (zone) of the earth, moving about as they please is not in consonance with the authentic traditions presented earlier which stated that, in general, the believers' souls are free to roam about in Paradise. The second part of this view, which claims that the disbelievers' souls are in *sijjīn* (the seventh earth), is not in consonance with the previously stated fact that the souls of the disbelievers are confined to and imprisoned in their graves. This concept concerning *sijjīn* is based on a weak narration whose text follows:

وروي أن ابن عباس سأل كعبا عن سجين وعليين فقال كعب: أما عليون فالسماء السابعة فيها أرواح المؤمنين، وأما سجين فالأرض السابعة السفلى، وأرواح الكفار تحت جسد إبليس

It has been related: "Ibn ʿAbbās asked Kaʿb [al-Aḥbār] about the meanings of the terms '*sijjīn*' and '*ʿilliyyūn*,' to which Kaʿb replied, 'As for "*ʿilliyyūn*," it designates the seventh heaven in which are the believers' souls. And as for "*sijjīn*," it indicates

245 See *ʿAqīdat al-Mu'min*, p. 401.

246 See *Kitāb al-Rūḥ*, pp. 146-147.

the seventh lowest earth; the souls of the disbeliever are under the body of Iblīs.'"[247]

As mentioned in the Qur'ān, the two terms "*ʿilliyyūn*" and "*sijjīn*" are the respective books[248] in which are written the records of the believers' and disbelievers' deeds. Thus, as indicated by the deeds recorded in these books, these terms designate the degree of the place prepared for each of the two categories of people, not the actual place where they will be. In light of this, the position expressed by some scholars in view number three is also untenable.

Imām Aḥmad is correct in stating that the souls of the believers are in Paradise (view number two). However, this view is correct only if it includes the stipulation that they are pious believers. As mentioned earlier, if they are sinful believers, they may have to spend an appointed term confined to the punishment and torment of their graves. Furthermore, his statement that the souls of the disbelievers are in the Fire is, correct only if the term "Fire" refers to the fire of their grave, in which they are tormented. They will not enter the fire of Hell (may Allāh protect us from it) until the Day of Judgement, after which they will become its inhabitants forever.

Finally, the opinion held by some companions and their followers (view number four) which states that the souls of the believers are with Allāh (without any elaboration) was probably due to their humility and modesty.[249] Moreover, the prevailing

---

[247] The *athar* is weak due to the unreliability of some of the narrators as well as a missing link in the chain of transmitters. Ibn Kathīr says that it is from the reports transmitted in Jewish traditions, termed "*isrā'īliyyāt.*" See his *tafsīr*, vol. 5, p. 236.

[248] Or according to some commentators, the places where these books are kept. See Sūrah al-*Muṭaffifīn*, 83:7-9 and 18-21.

[249] This is the best interpretation, for one should not imagine them to have been ignorant of the various verses and traditions which clarify this matter.

tendency of their era was not to dwell on a subject in which they felt their knowledge was limited. Some scholars who support this view sometimes quote the following *athar* (narration traced to a companion):

عن حذيفة بن اليمان قال: الأرواح موقوفة عند الرحمن عز وجل تنتظر موعده حتى ينفخ فيها

> Ḥudhayfah bin al- Yamān narrated.- "Souls are held with the Merciful [i.e., Allāh], the Almighty and Majestic, awaiting the appointed time when they will be resurrected to life."[250]

This narration is unacceptable as proof of view number four for two main reasons. Firstly, its *sanad* is weak.[251] Secondly, by asserting that all souls are held with Allāh, this ḥadīth contradicts the Qur'ān[252] and other authentic texts of the sunnah, which indicate that the souls of the believers are free to roam about in Paradise, while the souls of the disbelievers are confined to the various torments of the grave.

The preceding exposition of this issue has clarified the matter fully, leaving no confusion. In conclusion, it is obvious that the circumstances of the human soul between death and the Resurrection differ widely according to certain variables[253]

---

[250] Related by Ibn al-Qayyim with a weak *isnād*.

[251] Because of the extremely unreliable narrator Dāwūd bin Yazīd. For details, see Ibn Ḥajar's *Tahdhīb al-Tahdhīb*, vol. 3, p. 205.

[252] Such as the verse which states that Pharaoh's people are exposed to the fire in their graves morning and evening. See Sūrah *Ghāfir*, 40:46.

[253] Such as faith or disbelief, piety or sinfulness, debts, etc.

which determine their particular place and condition - which in themselves may change[254] or remain the same.[255]

[254] For example, the believer who has committed some major sins may be confined to the grave and its torment for a limited period and then be released to roam in Paradise. In any case, the freed believers' souls in Paradise are capable of instantaneous connection with their bodies and their graves. Their souls may meet and communicate with other souls of the dead and the sleeping.

[255] Such as the souls of disbelievers and sinful Muslims who are confined to the torture of their graves until the Resurrection.

The Soul's Faculties in the *Barzakh*

One often wonders about the soul's faculties in the *barzakh* (the stage between death and the Resurrection). Can it hear? Can it see? Does it have knowledge of certain things going on in the world? In order to answer these and other questions, one must carefully scrutinize the quality of the evidence presented in support of certain claims made by scholars in this field.

The Deceased's Faculty of Hearing

It is a common concept among scholars[256] and others that the dead in their graves have the faculty of hearing a visitor's greeting, his supplication, talk, etc. Such a concept is unfounded, for it has no proof from clear texts of the divine *sharī'ah*. In fact, it is in open contradiction to the unchallengeable texts of the Qur'ān and the authentic traditions of the Prophet (ﷺ) which deny the possibility of the dead possessing this faculty.

Proof from the Qur'ān and the Sunnah Negating It

There are two unequivocal texts from the Qur'ān which deny the possibility of the dead in their graves possessing the faculty of hearing. Allāh, the Blessed and Exalted, states:

---

256 Among those who erred in this matter are Ibn Abid-Dunyā, Ibn 'Abdul-Barr, al-Qurṭubī, Ibn al-Qayyim and al-Shanqīṭī.

إِنَّكَ لَا تُسْمِعُ ٱلْمَوْتَىٰ وَلَا تُسْمِعُ ٱلصُّمَّ ٱلدُّعَآءَ إِذَا وَلَّوْا۟ مُدْبِرِينَ

"Verily, you cannot make the dead hear and you cannot make the deaf hear the call when they turn their backs and retreat."[257]

وَمَا يَسْتَوِى ٱلْأَحْيَآءُ وَلَا ٱلْأَمْوَٰتُ ۚ إِنَّ ٱللَّهَ يُسْمِعُ مَن يَشَآءُ ۖ وَمَآ أَنتَ بِمُسْمِعٍ مَّن فِى ٱلْقُبُورِ ﴿٢٢﴾

"The living and the dead are not alike. Allāh makes whoever He wishes hear, but you cannot make those in their graves hear."[258]

In the first verse Allāh addresses His messenger, Muḥammad (ﷺ), reminding him that he cannot make the disbelievers hear his invitation to Islām, for they are like the dead, who do not hear either. In the second verse Allāh points to the difference between the living and the dead - they are not at all alike. He further clarifies to His prophet that he cannot make the rejecters of faith hear the message (for they are dead in heart and in spirit) any more than he can make those in their graves hear what is spoken to them![259]

Just as the Qur'ān denies the possibility of the deceased possessing the faculty of hearing, there are a number of texts in the sunnah which arrive at the same conclusion. One such ḥadīth follows:

عن ابن مسعود أن النبي (ﷺ) قال: إن لله ملائكة سياحين في الأرض، يبلغوني عن أمتي السلام

Ibn Mas'ūd reported that the Prophet (ﷺ) said: "Allāh has angels who travel about the earth; they [do and will] convey to me the peace greeting from my ummah."[260]

---

[257] Sūrah *al-Naml*, 27:80.

[258] Sūrah *Fāṭir*, 35:22.

[259] See *Tafsīr al-Ṭabarī*, vol. 21, p. 36 and al-Qurṭubī's *al-Jāmi'*, vol. 13, p. 232.

[260] Authentically related by Abū Dāwūd.

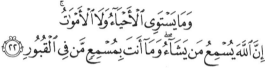

This ḥadīth clarifies that the Prophet (ﷺ) does not hear the greetings of peace from Muslims when they pronounce it upon him, for if he could hear it directly, there would be no need of angels to convey it to him. Therefore, it follows that the Prophet (ﷺ) cannot hear other forms of conversation directed at him either;[261] and it stands even more to reason that the deceased, being lesser than the Prophet (ﷺ), also cannot hear the *salām* (greeting of peace) or any other form of speech.[262] Thus, contrary to a popular misconception, because the Messenger (ﷺ) cannot directly hear either one's invocation of blessings[263] or one's *salām* addressed to him, such greetings may be conveyed to him from anywhere, regardless of the distance or proximity of the greeter to the Prophet's grave. The erroneous belief that the Prophet (ﷺ) hears these greetings directly disregards the previous ḥadīth which specifies that the greetings are conveyed to him by the angels, and it is based on a forged tradition whose text follows:

روي أن النبي (ﷺ) قال: من صلى علي عند قبري سمعته، ومن صلى علي نائيًا أبلغته

> It has been narrated that the Prophet (ﷺ) said. "Whoever asks blessings for me at my grave, I hear him, and whoever asks blessings upon me from afar, it is conveyed to me."[264]

---

261 Thus it is absolutely foolish for one to attempt to converse with the Prophet (ﷺ) or others at their graves. To ask them for any form of help is blatant *shirk*. Such is the misguidance spread by Sūfis, who have gone astray.

262 See *al-Āyāt al-Bayyināt* p. 37.

263 In Islām it is encouraged to invoke blessings upon the Prophet (ﷺ), and this commonly follows the mention of his name in one form or another.

264 This tradition was mentioned by al-ʿUqaylī in his book, *al-Ḍuʿafā* and by al-Khaṭīb, Ibn ʿAsākir, et. al., and they all agreed that it is a forged (*mawḍūʿ*) ḥadīth. See al-Albānī's *al-Aḥādīth al-Ḍaʿīfah*, Vol. 1, , ḥadīth no. 203.

Alleged Evidence and its Refutation

In order to refute allegations which claim that the deceased in the grave possess the faculty of hearing, it is essential to analyze them and discover the means by which such allegations are dependent upon weak and forged traditions and/or due to erroneous interpretations of various texts.

There are a number of authentic narrations relating the Prophet's address to the corpses of the *mushrikīn* (polytheists) of Quraysh who were slain by the believers in the Battle of Badr and then thrown into a dried well. The following two examples suffice for the purpose of the present discussion:

عن أبي طلحة أن نبي الله (ﷺ) أمر يوم بدر بأربعة وعشرين رجلا من صناديد قريش فقذفوا في طوى من أطواء بدر خبيث مخبث. فلما كان ببدر اليوم الثالث أمر براحلته فشد عليها رحلها، ثم مشى وأتبعه أصحابه وقالوا: ما نرى ينطلق إلا لبعض حاجته، حتى قام على شفة الركى فجعل يناديهم بأسمائهم وأسماء آبائهم: يا فلان بن فلان، ويا فلان بن فلان! أيسركم أنكم أطعتم الله ورسوله، فإنا قد وجدنا ما وعدنا ربنا حقا، فهل وجدتم ما وعد ربكم حقا؟ فقال عمر: يا رسول الله! ما تكلم من أجساد لا أرواح لها. وهل يسمعون؟ يقول الله عز وجل: ﴿إِنَّكَ لا تُسْمِعُ الْمَوْتَىٰ﴾؟ فقال رسول الله (ﷺ): والذي نفس محمد بيده، ما أنتم بأسمع لما أقول منهم. قال قتادة: أحياهم الله حتى أسمعهم قوله توبيخا، وتصغيرا، ونقمة، وحسرة، وندما.

Abū Ṭalḥah reported: "On the day of the Battle of Badr, Allāh's Prophet (ﷺ) ordered that the bodies of twenty-four leaders of the Quraysh be thrown into one of the foul, abandoned wells of Badr. On the third day after the battle the Prophet called for his mount and saddled it. Then he set out, so his companions followed him. They said among themselves, 'He must be going to something important.' When the Prophet (ﷺ) arrived at the Well,[265] he stood at its edge and began addressing those therein by calling upon them by their names, 'O so and so, son of so and so; and you, so and so, son of so and so! Would it not have been easier to have obeyed Allāh and His Messenger? We have found that which our Lord promised us to be true.[266] Did you find what your Lord promised you to be true?'[267] Thereupon 'Umar said , 'O Messenger of Allāh, what are you saying to these bodies without souls?! Do they hear? For Allāh, the Majestic and Mighty, says, "Verily, you cannot make the dead hear."[268] The Prophet (ﷺ) answered, 'By Him in whose hand lies the soul of Muḥammad, you did not hear better than them what I just said.'" Qatādah[269] added. "Allāh brought them[270] back to life [momentarily] in order to make them hear as a means of scorn and belittlement and [so that they would feel] regret and remorse."[271]

In another narration of this incident there is a slight variation in the wording of the text which follows:

عن ابن عمر قال: وقف النبي (ﷺ) على قليب بدر فقال:
هل وجدتم ما وعدكم ربكم حقا؟ فقال: إنهم الآن يسمعون

[265] Into which the bodies of the slain Quraysh had been thrown earlier.

[266] That is, that the believers would have victory over their enemy, the Quraysh. See al-Qurṭubī's *al-Jāmiʿu li Aḥkām al-Qur'ān,* vol. 7, p. 370 regarding the information about Sūrah *al-Anfāl*, 8:7-10.

[267] This is a reference to the Quraysh's supplication asking their Lord to bring a painful punishment upon them if what Muḥammad (ﷺ) was preaching was the truth. See Sūrah *al-Anfāl*, 8:32.

[268] Sūrah *al-Naml*, 27:80.

[269] A famous *tābiʿī* and a narrator of this ḥadīth.

[270] The slain Quraysh whose bodies were in the abandoned well.

[271] Authentically related by al-Bukhārī and Muslim.

ما أقول. فذكر لعائشة فقالت: إنما قال النبي (ﷺ): إنهم الآن يعلمون أن الذي كنت أقول لهم هو الحق. ثم قرأت ﴿إِنَّكَ لا تُسْمِعُ الْمَوْتَى﴾. حتى قرأت الاية.

Ibn ʿUmar related: "The Prophet (ﷺ) stood at the edge of a well[272] at Badr and said, 'Did you find the promise of your Lord to be true?'Then he added, 'Verily, at this moment they hear what I am saying.' Later on,[273] this was mentioned to ʿĀ'ishah,[274] whereupon she commented, 'What the Prophet (ﷺ) meant was, "Now they know that what I used to tell them is the truth."' Then she recited, 'Verily, you cannot make the dead hear,'[275] up to the end of the verse."[276]

Some often misconstrue the texts of the two aforementioned ḥadīths as proof for the contention that the dead can hear. However, the following argumentation refutes such a claim. This miraculous circumstance in which the corpses of the slain Quraysh were made to hear the Prophet's address to them is a special case - an exception to the general rule that the dead do not hear.[277] By a miracle, Allāh, the Almighty, made them hear the scolding from the Prophet (ﷺ) - only for the moment he spoke to them![278] This is clearly proven by the second narration itself, for their hearing was said to be conditioned by the moment when the Prophet (ﷺ)

---

[272] The same well mentioned earlier into which the bodies of the slain Quraysh were thrown.

[273] Most likely after the Prophet's death.

[274] The beloved wife of the Prophet.

[275] Sūrah *al-Naml*, 27:80.

[276] Related by al-Bukhārī and others with an authentic chain of transmitters.

[277] See al-Ālūsī's *Rūḥ al-Maʿānī*, vol. 6, p. 455.

[278] This is confirmed by many of the dependable commentators and jurists. For example, see *al-Āyāt al-Bayyināt*, pp. 29, 56 and 59.

called out to them in scorn and rebuke. He said, "At this moment they hear what I am saying." Furthermore, in the first narration the Prophet (ﷺ) does not deny 'Umar's sound understanding of the verse's general ruling that the dead do not hear. Rather, the Prophet (ﷺ) merely clarifies for 'Umar that what occurred at Badr was a divine miracle and, therefore, an exception to the general ruling of the verse.[279]

Another text often quoted by those who believe that the dead can hear is the following tradition:

> عن أنس بن مالك أن رسول الله (ﷺ) قال: إن العبد إذا وضع في قبره، وتولى عنه أصحابه إنه ليسمع قرع نعالهم إذا انصرفوا، أتاه الملكان
>
> Anas bin Mālik reported that Allāh's Messenger (ﷺ) said. "After the deceased is placed in his grave and his companions[280] turn to leave, he hears the shuffling of their feet as they walk away. Then there comes to him the two angels."[281]

This text is not valid evidence for the general claim that the dead can hear; rather, this tradition only specifies another exception to the general rule. In this case, the deceased hears the shuffling feet of those who attended his funeral as they walk away. This is a momentary possession of the faculty of hearing which is terminated at the point at which the two questioning angels[282] come to him.[283]

---

[279] See *al-Āyāt al-Bayyināt*, pp. 30-31.

[280] His friends and others who attended his burial.

[281] For the full text of this compilation of several, authentic hadīths related by al-Bukhārī and Muslim, see pp. 30-42.

[282] Their names are Munkar and Nakīr, and their fearful appearance has been described earlier in this treatise.

[283] See *al-Āyāt al-Bayyināt*, pp. 38 and 56.

From what has preceded, it is abundantly clear that the deceased generally do not have the faculty of hearing, for they are beyond the barrier (*barzakh*) which separates our world from theirs. This proves the gross error in the thinking of those who attempt to carry on "conversations" with the dead, or worse, petition them for certain things. Petitioning the dead is *shirk*, and this is indeed the greatest of all sins.

The Deceased's Faculty of Recognition

Just as there are proponents of the theory that the deceased can hear in the grave, there are those who claim that the dead can recognise visitors at the grave as well. The following text is presented as evidence by the proponents of such a theory to support their claim:

روي عن النبي (ﷺ) أنه قال: ما من أحد يمر بقبر أخيه المؤمن كان يعرفه في الدنيا فسلم عليه إلا عرفه ورد عليه

> It has been related that the Prophet (ﷺ) said: "Anyone who passes by the grave of his fellow believer [whom he knew in this world] and pronounces the peace greeting upon him will be recognised by the deceased, and his greeting will be returned."[284]

This tradition does not stand as a valid piece of evidence because it is *munkar*(rejectable). In their quest to acquire as much proof as possible, the proponents of the theory that the deceased can recognise people from the grave often use traditions which are rejected by the scholars of Islām. These traditions are, for the most part, either weak or forged and, therefore, cannot be used as evidence to support their claims.[285]

---

[284] Mentioned by Ibn Rajab in his *Aḥwāl al-Qubūr* and al-Albānī in his *Silsilat al-Aḥadīth al-Ḍaʿīfah*, ḥadīth no. 4493.

[285] The scope of this study does not permit mentioning these in detail. Whoever wishes to be acquainted with them can see al-Ālūsī's treatise, *al-Āyāt al-Bayyināt*, in which a good number of them are mentioned.

Some may say that if the dead cannot hear, then there is no point in greeting them at their graves as has been mentioned in the authentic sunnah. In reply, to show the wisdom in and meaning of the peace greeting addressed to the deceased in their graves, the text of one of these traditions[286] is quoted as follows:

عن بريدة قال: كان رسول الله (ﷺ) يعلمهم إذا خرجوا إلى المقابر: السلام عليكم أهل الديار من المؤمنين والمسلمين، وإنا إن شاء الله بكم لاحقون، أسأل الله لنا ولكم العافية

Buraydah narrated: "Allāh's Messenger (ﷺ) used to teach the people [what to say] when they went to visit the graves: 'Peace be upon you, O people of these dwellings from [among] the Muslims and believers.[287] Allāh-willing,[288] we shall be joining you. I ask Allāh's forgiveness for all of us and for you.'"[289]

This greeting of peace to the dead is a supplication - a prayer for the deceased on the part of the visitor. The meaning can be understood in the following words: "May the peace, mercy and forgiveness of Allāh be upon you, O inhabitants[290] of these graves!" The greeting is a request for *salām* which connotes safety, peace, contentment

---

286 The words vary but they are all similar in meaning as well as in intent.

287 In Arabic, "*mu'minīn.*" It is used here to differentiate between the degree of faith and practice of those who are Muslim. A *mu'min* (singular) is a true and deeply faithful follower of Islām. A Muslim is anyone who pronounces the declaration of faith. Thus, every *mu'min* is a Muslim but not necessarily vice-versa.

288 The reason he says, "Allāh-willing" is that, in essence, he cannot guarantee his own dying in faith as a Muslim or a *mu'min*. Ultimately, that is up to Allāh. This is actually a *du'ā* asking Allāh to let him die as a believer in Islām.

289 Related by Muslim, al-Nasā'ī, et. al. with an authentic chain of transmitters.

290 This is restricted to the deceased Muslims in their graves and is not to be addressed to the graves of disbelievers.

and rest. Such can only come about by Allāh's forgiveness and mercy for the deceased Muslim who is confined in the grave. Even if the soul is in Paradise, the greeting is still a supplication and a blessing. Needless to say, such a greeting does not presuppose that the inhabitants "hear" it or respond to it.

In conclusion, neither does one in the grave "see" who is visiting, nor does one have the knowledge thereof. No authentic texts of the divine *sharī'ah* support such a notion. All that has been related in this area is either weak or forged[291] or is the misinterpretation of some scholars. Such bears no weight at all in matters of *dīn*, which can only be valid if based on authentic, divinely related proof.[292]

The Deceased's Knowledge of Earthly Affairs

There exist a number of traditions and *āthār* (narrations traced to the companions or their followers) which indicate that the dead person's soul is brought news of worldly affairs and even the minutest details of others' lives. However, all of these are weak and invalid. The following is an example of such:

روي عن ابن مسعود أن النبي (ﷺ) قال: حياتي خير لكم، ومماتي خير لكم، تعرض علي أعمالكم، فما رأيت من خير حمدت الله عليه، وما رأيت من شر استغفرت الله لكم. وفي رواية عن أنس: تعرض علي أعمالكم كل خميس

It has been related that Ibn Mas'ūd reported that the Prophet (ﷺ) said. "My life is good for you and my death is also, for your deeds are shown to me. Whatever I see of good [deeds],

---

[291] See *Kitāb al-Rūḥ*, pp. 12-21, especially the footnotes which affirm the weakness of all of these traditions.

[292] Opinions of scholars on such speculative matters are not considered as *'aqīdah* in any case. (ed.)

> I praise Allāh for that. And whatever I see of evil [deeds], I ask Allāh's forgiveness for you."[293] [And in a narration traced back to Anas: "Your deeds are displayed for me every Thursday."][294]

Both of these narrations regarding the Prophet himself (ﷺ) are rejectable. The first one was transmitted by weak chains of narrators, while the second one contains a transmitter who is known to have forged traditions.[295] Furthermore, the meaning of these texts conflicts with other texts of the divine *sharīʿah* and contradicts sound reasoning. There are a number of authentically related traditions whose texts clearly stipulate that the Prophet (ﷺ) has no knowledge of the condition and circumstances of his followers after his death. Among these are the narrations regarding the Prophet's pond (*ḥawḍ*)[296] such as the following:

> عن عائشة رضي الله عنها قالت: سمعت رسول الله (ﷺ) يقول: إني على الحوض أنظر من يرد علي منكم، فوالله ليقتطعن دوني رجال، فلأقولن: أي رب، مني ومن أمتي، فيقول: إنك لاتدري ما عملوا بعدك، ما زالوا يرجعون على أعقابهم

> ʿĀ'ishah (may Allāh be pleased with her) related. "I heard Allāh's Messenger (ﷺ) say, 'I will be at the pond, looking at those of you who come to me. Then, by Allāh, some men will be removed from me, whereupon I will say, "O my Lord, they are from my *Ummah*." But He will say, "Verily, you do

---

[293] Related by al-Bazzār, et. al. with a weak *sanad*.

[294] A forged tradition related by Abū Ṭāhir al-Mukhlis. See al-Albānī's *Silsilat al-Aḥadīth al-Ḍaʿīfah*, vol. 2, ḥadīth no. 975.

[295] See *Silsilat al-Aḥadīth al-Ḍaʿīfah*, vol. 2, p. 407.

[296] A watering place which the blessed will drink from on the Day of Reckoning. Its water is whiter than milk and sweeter than honey. Whoever drinks of it will never thirst thereafter. This has been related in an authentic ḥadīth in Muslim's compilation.

> not know what they did after you; they continued backsliding, turning back on their heels.""'"[297]

If the Prophet (ﷺ) had been shown the deeds of his followers, it would not have been said to him in the preceding ḥadīth, "Verily, you do no know what they did after you." Furthermore, one questions the purpose in his being shown his follower's deeds, since he is not responsible for them. The Qur'ān states:

وَلَا تَزِرُ وَازِرَةٌ وِزْرَ أُخْرَىٰ

"No soul shall bear the burden of another."[298]

Surely, it is not in consonance with Allāh's infinite justice and wisdom that He cause torment and pain to His most beloved messenger, Muḥammad (ﷺ), by showing him the evil deeds of the followers who disobeyed him after his death. Would such painful revelations not remove whatever pleasures and joys the Prophet (ﷺ) is to enjoy in the *barzakh*?[299] Obviously, such a concept is unacceptable, considering the exalted relationship between Allāh and His final, chosen messenger.

The preceding argument is true for other members of the Muslim *ummah* as well. The narrations attributed to the companions and their followers intimating that the dead person is informed of the most minute details of the affairs of his former household, family, friends, etc. are all weak and unacceptable.[300] Moreover, why should a pious person be grieved and tormented

---

[297] Related by Muslim, et. al. They "turned back on their heels" in that they returned to their old evil ways of sin, while some of them might even have turned away from Islām.

[298] Sūrah *al-Isrā'*, 17:15.

[299] For more details disproving this erroneous concept, see Muḥammad Khaleel al-Harrās's commentary, *Sharḥ al-Qaṣeedat al-Nūniyyah*, vol. 2, pp. 20-21

[300] For a sample of these, see Ibn al-Qayyim's *Kitāb al-Rūḥ*, pp. 12-21.

by the news of the misfortunes and deeds of his impious family members. Surely, that would be unjust, and Allāh, the Just, is exalted above all defects and shortcomings, which are not in consonance with His infinate completeness and perfection.

In conclusion, it is obvious that the faculties of the dead regarding earthly affairs during the period of the *barzakh* are very limited. However, it might be asked: "Since it was previously mentioned in certain traditions that the souls of the sleeping are able to converse with the souls of the dead, and that they are asked by the latter about news from the earth, then can they not also have certain knowledge of earthly affairs, their family, etc.?" In keeping with the previous arguments presented, the "news" which they receive is limited in content and rare in occurrence. Moreover, the nature of this type of news would not be such that the souls of the deceased are troubled or tormented by such information.

The State of the body in the Grave

The changes which the body and the soul undergo upon death have already been mentioned along with the manner in which the soul is extracted from the body according to its faith and deeds. The circumstances of the soul feel the pleasure or the torment of the grave? What happens to physical body? How long do the respective states of torment or pleasure remain? In order to answer these and other questions, one must carefully scrutinize the available information and come to a conclusion based upon the texts of the Qur'ān and the sunnah, logic and sound reasoning.

The State of the Physical Body in the Grave

The physical body of the deceased must decompose in the grave and eventually perish.[301] This is the general ruling for all mankind except those which will be discussed shortly. This principle is supported by a number of authentic traditions such as the following:

عن أبي هريرة أن رسول الله (ﷺ) قال: كل ابن آدم يأكله التراب إلا عجب الذنب، منه خلق وفيه يركب. وفي رواية: إن في الإنسان عظما لا تأكله الأرض أبدا. فيه يركب يوم القيامة

[301] Even if a body is mummified, kept in a chemical solution or otherwise artificially maintained.

Abū Hurayrah reported that Allāh's Messenger (ﷺ) said: "All of Ādam's progeny will be eaten by the soil except for [that portion of his body which is called] "ajb adh-dhanab'; for man was created from it, and he will be reassembled from it." [And in another narration: "Verily in man there is a bone which the earth will never eat up; from it he will be reassembled on the Day of Resurrection."][302]

From these traditions it is clear that the earth causes the body to decompose, thereby "eating it up" until eventually nothing remains except the portion of the skeleton called "*'ajb adh-dhanab.*"[303] This term refers to a small piece of the tailbone at the base of the spine. It is described further in another narration:

قيل يا رسول الله، ما عجب الذنب؟ قال: مثل حبة خردل، منه ينبتون

"Allāh's Messenger (ﷺ) was questioned, 'What is the *'ajb adh-dhanab*?' He answered, 'It is like a mustard seed; from it the bodies grow [back to their original forms].'"[304]

According to the commentators of ḥadīth,[305] the divine wisdom in making this tiny point resistant to decomposition is that Allāh (glorified be His Majesty and Power) designated this *'ajb* as a sign for the angels that they may revive every human as he was. By leaving each person's *'ajb* intact, the angels know which souls

---

[302] These two narrations were compiled by Muslim with dependable chains of transmitters. Similar traditions have been related by al-Bukhārī, Aḥmad, et. al.

[303] In some narrations the wording is "*'ajm,*" using the letter "*mīm*" instead of the letter "*bā.*" However, the meaning remains the same. See *Ṣaḥīfat Humām bin Munabbih*, p. 274; *Fatḥ al-Bāri*, vol. 8, p.552 and *al-Musnad*, vol. 16, p. 71.

[304] Related by al-Ḥākim, Abū Ya'lā, et. al. with a dependable *isnād*.

[305] See, for example, '*Umdah al-Qāri*', vol. 15, pp. 412-413 and *Awjaz al-Masālik ilā Muwaṭṭa' Mālik*, vol. 4, pp. 293-294.

should be returned to which individuals. This concept can be understood through the Qur'ānic example of a man who died along with his donkey.[306] The bones of the latter remained intact in order that Allāh might dress them with flesh and bring them back to life to indicate that the revived donkey was the man's very same donkey and not another. Thus, without remnants of the original bodies it would be possible for the angels to return the souls to other bodies, not necessarily the very bodies from which they were separated at death and to which they must be rejoined for the Resurrection and Judgement.[307]

In contrast to the bodies of disbelievers and most believers, the bodies of the prophets and messengers of Allāh are preserved intact, and the earth is prevented from having any effect upon them. This is proven by authentic traditions of the Prophet (ﷺ), an example of which follows:

عن أوس بن أوس أن النبي (ﷺ) قال: من أفضل أيامكم يوم الجمعة، فيه خلق الله آدم، وفيه قبض وفيه النفخة وفيه الصعقة؛ فأكثروا علي من الصلاة فإن صلاتكم معروضة علي. قالوا: يا رسول الله، و كيف تعرض عليك صلاتنا وقد أرمت؟ قال: إن الله حرم على الأرض أن تأكل أجساد الأنبياء

Aws bin Aws related: "The Prophet (ﷺ) said, 'The day of *Jumu'ah* [Friday] is one of your best days. On this day Allāh created Ādam and caused him to die thereon. Furthermore,

---

[306] See Sūrah *al-Baqarah*, 2:259. A man passed by an abandoned village in utter ruins. He wondered, "How will Allāh revive this after its death [i.e., ruin]?" So Allāh caused him to die and after 100 years raised him up. The man thought that he had tarried only a day or a portion thereof but was told to look at his food (which remained unchanged) and at his donkey (which was only a pile of bones). Finally, the bones of the donkey were brought together and clothed with flesh before his very eyes.

[307] See *Fatḥ al-Bāri*, vol. 8, p. 553.

> the *nafkhah* and *ṣāʿiqah*[308] occur on this day. So invoke blessings[309] upon me, for verily your invocation is conveyed to me.' The companions asked, 'O Messenger of Allāh, how will our invocation be conveyed to you when you will have decomposed?' He replied, 'Verily, Allāh has forbidden the earth to eat the bodies of the prophets.'"[310]

This tradition clearly states that the prophets' bodies are protected from decomposing as a special exception to the general rule that human bodies (except for the *ʿajb adh-dhanab*, as mentioned earlier) rot and are spoiled by the earth. However, one should not understand from this text that the prophets are "alive,"[311] as has been misconstrued by some of the misguided Sufis and some simple-minded people.[312] Such a misconception (along with others of a similar nature) has led them to commit *shirk* by addressing the prophets in their graves.[313]

---

[308] These two terms are referred to in the Qur'ān in Sūrah *al-Zumar*,39:68. The term "*ṣāʿiqah*" literally means "a thunderbolt" but here it indicates that deafening blast which will kill all who exist in the heavens and on the earth except whom Allāh wills of His creation. This occurs just before the Resurrection. The term "*nafkhah*" means "a gust of air or breath." Here it indicates the blowing of the trumpet whereupon souls will be resurrected and rise to meet their Lord for the Judgement. See *al-Iṣfahānī's Muʿjam Alfāẓ Mufradāt al-Qur'ān,* pp. 289 and 523.

[309] Indicates the familiar formula which is recited in asking Allāh for blessings and bounties upon the Prophet

[310] Authentically related by al-Ḥākim, Ibn Ḥibbān, et. al.

[311] They are not "alive" with a worldly life. Their "life" is that of the *barzakh,* which differs from that of this world.

[312] See Muḥammad Khaleel al-Harrās's *Sharḥ al-Qaṣīdat al-Nūniyyah,* vol. 2, pp. 6-7 and al-Ālūsī's *al-Āyāt al-Bayyināt*, pp. 76-80.

[313] Their "proof" that the Prophet (ﷺ) is alive in his grave is that they "talk" to him at his grave, ask for his help and call upon him for aid and assistance. All of these are clear, open acts of *shirk*. May Allāh protect us from such obvious ensnarements of Satan.

It is a commonly held that others besides the prophets also share this special favour, i.e., their bodies are protected from the earth after burial. However, there is no dependable text affirming this. Among those mistakenly included with the category of prophets are the martyrs and the *mu'adhdhins* (callers to prayer), who seek their reward solely from Allāh.[314] Still others included the *ṣiddīqūn* (literally, "the truthful and righteous"), the practicing scholars, the memorisers of Qur'ān who practice its directives, the *murābits* (the warriors who remain in readiness for battle), those who die of plague in patience expecting reward, those who constantly pronounce Allāh's praises (*dhikr*) and those who love Allāh sincerely.[315]

There are no clear texts authentically related by the Prophet (ﷺ) which state that the bodies of the martyrs are prevented from decomposing as are those of the prophets of Allāh. However, there have been reports by *tābiʿīn* indicating that the bodies of the martyred companions had been witnessed years after their deaths and that they appeared as if just buried.[316] Countless people of various generations also have claimed to have seen the bodies of martyrs intact in their graves. It would be foolish to deny constantly recurring reports which attest to this fact.[317] Ibn Abul-ʿIzz, the commentator of *al-Ṭaḥāwiyyah*, further affirms this phenomenon, saying, "As for martyrs, their bodies have been witnessed intact

---

[314] This category was added by al-Qurṭubī in his book, *al-Tadhkirah*, p. 164.

[315] These categories were mentioned by al-Zurqānī and quoted by al-Kandahlāwī in his ḥadīth commentary entitled *Awjaz al Masālik*, vol. 4, p. 294.

[316] Mālik relates one such incident, but the *sanad* has some missing links. However, the ḥadīth scholar, Ibn ʿAbdul-Barr, claims that this narration has been reported with other authentic, connected chains of transmitters. See *al-Tadhkirah*, p. 163.

[317] The occurrence of eyewitness reports has been mentioned and affirmed by al-Qayyim as well. See *Sharḥ al-Qaṣīdat al-Nūniyyah,* vol. 2, pp. 13-14.

in their graves after long periods of time. It is possible that a martyr's body remains intact until the Resurrection, just as it is quite possible that it remains sound for only a long period of time; and (verily, Allāh knows best) perhaps, the more perfect one's martyrdom was, the longer his body remains intact."[318]

In contrast to the category of martyrs, the other aforementioned categories must be outright rejected because the claims stating that the bodies of such people do not deteriorate in their graves are based upon weak narrations or mere conjecture or appear to be deduced by analogy. Such methods of deduction are rejected, for there is agreement among the dependable scholars of *ahl al-sunnah* that analogy cannot be applied in matters relating to *ʿaqīdah*. As for mere conjecture, it avails nothing of the truth,[319] rather, it is the most deceptive of all discourse.[320]

The Torment or Pleasure of the grave

The scholars of Islām differed concerning the torment or pleasure of the grave. Some were of the opinion that the torment or pleasure is felt by only the body, whereas others stated that it is felt by both the body and the soul together. Still others insisted that it is the soul alone which feels torment or pleasure. Shaykh al-Islām Ibn Taymiyyah discusses these issues in his monumental *Majmūʿ al-Fatāwā*.[321] He mentions the proponents of the various contradicting views[322] as well as the fact that all of these opinions have elements of error. The only correct view is that of *ahl al-*

---

[318] See *Sharḥ al-ʿAqīdat al-Ṭaḥāwiyyah,* p. 456.

[319] Stated in Sūrah *al-Najm*, 53:28.

[320] According to the authentically related tradition of al-Bukhārī and Muslim

[321] Vol. 4, pp. 282-299.

[322] Ibid., pp. 283-284.

sunnah wa al-jamāʿah, who unanimously agree that the torment or pleasure of the grave is experienced by both the body and the soul together. The soul may feel one of these two states while it is either separated from or connected to the body.[323]

It has already been mentioned[324] that the soul is returned to the body in the grave for questioning. In the case of the disbeliever, the grave closes in on the body, squeezing the rib cage so tightly that it cracks and the ribs of the right side enter between those of the left. The fact that the soul returns to the body for questioning at this time proves that the torment is experienced by both the body and the soul together. The Prophet (ﷺ) was also shown the torment of sinful believers in the grave - both their bodies and souls received various punishments, commensurate with their heinous crimes and transgressions. Thus, it is clear that the soul and the body together experience the effect of torment or pleasure, not just one or the other as some have erroneously contended.[325]

The Length of the Respective States of Torment and Pleasure

It has been mentioned that the two respective states of torment and pleasure are felt by both the body and the soul together and

---

[323] The soul is only separate from the body if it is that of the pious believer in Paradise, for the soul is experiencing pleasure there while the body is enjoying pleasure in the grave. Moreover, when the soul wishes to connect with the body in the grave, pleasure is achieved for both the body and soul together. As for the disbeliever, the foul soul is confined to the lowly depths of the grave where it is punished and tormented along with the body.

[324] In a previous section entitled: "The Taking of the Soul and the State of the Grave."

[325] See *Sharḥ al-Ṭaḥāwiyyah,* p. 451 and *Lawāmiʿ al-Anwār*, vol. 2, p. 24.

in the case of the pious believer, separately as well. But one may ask what happens to a person's body if it is partially or utterly destroyed due to an accident and is not buried in the earth. The scholars of old discussed this problem, resulting in the dependable view as stated by Ibn al-Qayyim: "It should be known that the torment of the grave is the torment of the *barzakh*; thus, everyone who dies and deserves to be punished must taste his portion thereof, whether he was buried in a grave or not. Consequently, if a person was eaten by a predator, burnt in a fire until he became ashes, blown up in the sky and scattered, or drowned in the sea, his designated punishment would reach his body [and soul], just as it reaches those in their graves."[326] The opposite can be applied to the pious believer whose body was similarly destroyed - pleasure will reach the body and soul no matter where it is scattered or placed. Such a thing is easy for Allāh, who is able to do as He wills. Moreover, such a thing is in consonance with divine justice, otherwise, the foul sinner or rejecting disbeliever could be spared the full torment which is due on both the body and the soul, while the pious believer might not taste the full pleasure which is also due.

---

[326] See *Kitāb al-Rūḥ*, p. 84.

The State of the Soul upon Termination of the *Barzakh*

What has preceded constitutes a discussion of the soul's condition during sleep and upon death and its circumstances in the *barzakh*. However, this discussion would not be complete without an analysis of the state of the soul upon termination of the *barzakh*. The limited scope of this study permits only a brief summary of the pertinent data relating to this issue.

The Resurrection of Bodies and Souls

On the Day of Judgement the trumpet will be blown with such a resounding thunder that all creatures of the heavens and the earth will die except whom Allāh wills.[327] This has been mentioned in numerous Qur'ānic verses[328] such as the following:

وَيَوۡمَ يُنفَخُ فِي ٱلصُّورِ فَفَزِعَ مَن فِي ٱلسَّمَٰوَٰتِ وَمَن فِي
ٱلۡأَرۡضِ إِلَّا مَن شَآءَ ٱللَّهُۚ وَكُلٌّ أَتَوۡهُ دَٰخِرِينَ ٨٧

---

[327] The exception referred to is a point of difference between the scholars. It is said by some that the reference is to martyrs, while others say it refers to the prophets, *al-ḥūr al-ʿayn* (the women of Paradise) or the general body of believers. Even others say it is a reference to the angels, e.g., Jibrīl, Mīka'īl, The Angel of Death, the carriers of the Throne, etc. Perhaps the soundest view is that all of these together are correct. See a detailed discussion of the issue in al-Qurṭubī's *tafsīr al-Jāmiʿ*, vol. 13, pp. 240-241 and vol. 15, pp. 279-280.

[328] See also Sūrah *al-Zumar*, 39:68.

"On that day the trumpet will be blown which will shock [to death] whoever is in the heavens and on the earth except whom Allāh wills. And all will come unto Him humbly."[329]

Human bodies will unite with their souls and emerge from their graves, proceeding to meet their Lord. The following verses describe this reality clearly:

وَنُفِخَ فِي ٱلصُّورِ فَإِذَا هُم مِّنَ ٱلْأَجْدَاثِ إِلَىٰ رَبِّهِمْ يَنسِلُونَ ﴿٥١﴾ قَالُوا۟ يَٰوَيْلَنَا مَنۢ بَعَثَنَا مِن مَّرْقَدِنَا ۜ ۗ هَٰذَا مَا وَعَدَ ٱلرَّحْمَٰنُ وَصَدَقَ ٱلْمُرْسَلُونَ ﴿٥٢﴾

"And the horn will be blown, then [immediately] they will hasten from their graves to their Lord. They will say, 'O ruined are we! Who has raised us up again from our beds?' [It will be said], 'This is what the Most Merciful had promised, and the messengers have spoken the truth.'"[330]

Once they arrive before Allāh, the process of judgement will begin.[331] In the end it is either to the pleasures of Paradise[332] or to the torments of Hell.[333] They will be in one of these two places with their bodies and souls united. Thus, the pious believers will have the full pleasure allotted to them by Allāh according to their degree of faith and righteous deeds acquired during their earthly

---

[329] Sūrah *al-Naml*, 27:87.

[330] Sūrah *Yā-Sīn*, 36:51-52. See also Sūrah *al-Qamar*, 54:7.

[331] This subject of the judgement and what occurs therein cannot be dealt with in this treatise. Whoever wishes to delve into the matter should see al-Qurṭubī's *al-Tadhkirah fī Aḥwāl al-Mawtā wa Umūr al-Ākhirah* and *Lawāmi' al-Anwār*.

[332] For an excellent study of what Paradise is like and what wonderful pleasures are in store for the pious believer, see Ibn al-Qayyim's *Ḥādī al-Arwāḥ ilā Bilād al-Afrāḥ*.

[333] For a detailed description thereof, see Ibn Rajab's *al-Takhwīf min al-Nār*.

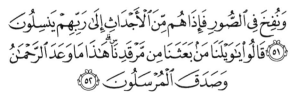

existence. Similarly, the truly sinful Muslims and the disbelievers, who rejected faith, will have the Fire for an abode. Sinful Muslims will spend a certain term of torment in the Fire in order to be purified of their transgressions against Allāh or humanity. If they believed in the oneness of Allāh and the final messengership of Muḥammad (ﷺ) but disobeyed their Creator's commands, they will be allowed to enter Paradise after this purification, as is narrated in an authentic tradition of Imām Muslim. As for the rejecters of Islām, they are doomed to eternal punishment in the everlasting torment of Hell (may Allāh protect us from it).

As can be surmised from the previous information, the soul is immortal and never dies or ceases to exist, for it was created to be eternal. The body, however, dies after its earthly existence has ended. Some scholars alleged that the soul also dies or becomes extinct because of the Qur'ānic verse which states that كُلُّ نَفْسٍ ذَآئِقَةُ ٱلْمَوْتِ "every soul will taste death."[334] The reply is that the soul tastes death at the time of the human body's decease, when the soul exits from the body. This is the extent of the soul's "death." The claim that the soul becomes extinct and vanishes completely is refuted by previously mentioned texts which clearly indicate that the soul is eternal,[335] either in Paradise or in Hell.

Even Death Must Die

Finally, since there is no further need for death after the Final Judgement, even death must die. For that reason it is slaughtered between Paradise and Hell as has been mentioned in a number of authentic traditions, some of which follow:

---

[334] As mentioned in the following places in the Qur'ān: Sūrah *Āl ʿImrān* 3: 185; Sūrah *al-Anbiyā'*, 21:35 and Sūrah *al-ʿAnkabūt*, 29:57.

[335] See *Kitāb al-Rūḥ*, pp. 51-52 and *Lawāmi' al-Anwar*; vol. 2, p. 38.

عن أبي هريرة أن رسول الله (ﷺ) قال: إذا دخل أهل الجنة الجنة وأهل النار النار أتي بالموت ملببا [كأنه كبش أملح] فيوقف على السور الذي بين أهل الجنة وأهل النار، ثم يقال: يا أهل الجنة! فيطلعون خائفين. ثم يقال: ياأهل النار فيطلعون مستبشرين، يرجون الشفاعة. فيقال لأهل الجنة ولأهل النار: هل تعرفون هذا؟ فيقول هؤلاء وهؤلاء: قد عرفناه، هو الموت الذي وكل بنا: فيضجع فيذبح ذبحا على السور، ثم يقال: يا أهل الجنة خلود لا موت، ويا أهل النار خلود لا موت

Abū Hurayrah reported that Allāh's Messenger said, "After the people of Paradise enter Paradise and the people of the fire enter Hell, death will be brought forward [i.e., grasped at the throat] in the form of a spotted ram.[336] It will be on the wall which separates the people of Paradise from the people of the Fire. Then it will be said, 'O people of Paradise!' Thereupon they will raise their heads and stare apprehensively.[337] Then it will be said, 'O people of the Fire,' whereupon its inhabitants will raise their heads in hope of intercession.[338] After this the people of Paradise and the inhabitants of the fire will be addressed thus, 'Do you know what this is?' They will all reply, 'We know it; it is death, which was assigned to us.' Thereupon death [in the form of the ram] will be placed on its side and slaughtered on the wall.[339] Finally, it will be said, 'O

---

[336] The Arabic term is "*amlaḥ*," which means "spotted with black and white." It is said that the reason for this choice of black and white is that the former colour indicates the description of the inhabitants of Hell, while the latter refers to the people of Paradise. See *Tuḥfah al-Aḥwāḍ* vol. 7, p. 278.

[337] The, fear that perhaps, they might be taken out of their pleasant abode.

[338] Hoping that they will be taken out of their painful abode.

[339] The wisdom behind this slaughtering of death is to impress upon the people of Paradise and the inhabitants of the Fire that their respective abodes are eternal. See *Fatḥ al-Bāri*, vol. 11, p. 421.

people of Paradise, [there is] only eternity and no more death. O people of the Fire, only eternity and no more death.'"[340]

[340] Authentically related by al-Bukhārī, Muslim and al-Tirmidhī.

Conclusion

The preceding discussion of the nature and circumstances of the human soul represents the Islāmic view regarding this very important subject, supported by the texts of the glorious Qur'ān and the authentic sunnah of the final messenger of Allāh, Muḥammad (ﷺ). It is trusted that the reader has derived benefit and understanding from the information contained herein. I pray that it provides food for thought and encourages the reflection on one's own life, one's faith, one's deeds and one's death, which surely must come. Finally, it is hoped that the reader will be moved to positive action in his or her own life. May we sincerely subscribe to faith in the one and only Creator and Lord, adhering to the principle of *tawhīd* and meticulously applying the divine guidance of Islām as embodied in the sunnah. This is the sole sure method of gaining Allāh's pleasure, the result of which is the bliss of Paradise and protection from the fire of Hell.

Glossary

ʿAjb adh-Dhanab: The root or base of the tailbone containing the seed from which man will be recreated in the next life.

ʿAllāmah: A title meaning "learned scholar."

ʿAqīdah: Belief, doctrine or creed.

Barzakh: The period between death and the Resurrection. Literally, "a partition or separation."

Daʿwah: A call, appeal or invitation to the path of Allāh. The propagation of Islām. Also, supplication or calling upon Allāh.

Dīn: Religion or way of life.

Dhikr: The remembrance of Allāh in the heart and on one's tongue.

Duʿā: Supplication to Allāh. An informal prayer.

Dunyā: The world or worldly affairs.

Fitnah: An affliction by which one is tried or tested. Temptation, conflict, a crime or madness. Something which misleads. Literally, "burning or melting (metals) in fire."

Ḥadīth: A saying of or about Prophet Muḥammad (ﷺ).

Ḥajj: One of the five pillars of Islām consisting of the pilgrimage to Makkah.

Ḥasan: The grade of a ḥadīth indicating that it is of good, acceptable quality.

Iblīs: The proper name of Satan.

Ibrāhīm: Abraham.

Isnād: The chain of transmitters of prophetic traditions.

Isrā': The Night Journey, referring specifically to the journey of Prophet Muḥammad (ﷺ) from the Sacred Mosque in Makkah to the Aqṣā Mosque in Jerusalem.

Jibrīl: Gabriel, the angel who conveyed revelation from Allāh,

Jihād: An effort or struggle in the path of Allāh by various means, including individual efforts in propagation and reform, and military efforts; when necessary. Literally, "effort or exertion."

Jinn: (Singular - *Jinnī*) Creatures unseen by man, created from fire and inhabiting the earth. Like man, they have been given a free will.

Kāfir: One who conceals his instinctive belief in Allāh. A disbeliever, denier or ungrateful one. Literally, "one who covers or conceals" (such as a planter of seeds).

Mīḵa'īl: Michael, the angel in charge of rain, plants and mercy.

Mi'rāj: The Ascension, referring specifically to the ascension of Prophet Muḥammad (ﷺ) from the Aqṣā Mosque to the heavens.

Mursal: A category of weakness in ḥadīth science.

Nafs: The soul or self.

Al-Qur'ān al-Karīm: The words of Allāh revealed to Muḥammad (ﷺ) the recital of which is an act of worship.

Ramaḍān: The ninth month of the Islāmic calendar during which the Muslims fast from dawn until sunset.

Rūḥ: The soul or spirit.

Ṣaḥīḥ: The grade of a ḥadīth indicating that it is authentic, supported by a continuous chain of trusted narrators. Literally, "correct or accurate."

Sanad: The authenticity of a ḥadīth derived from its chain of narrators (*isnād*). Literally, "support."

Sharī'ah: The divinely revealed laws found in the Qur'ān and the sunnah. Literally, "the path or way."

Shaykh: An elder, a man of authority, a leader or a learned man.

Shaykh al-Islām: A title given to the prominent scholar of a certain era, such as Aḥmad bin Taymiyyah.

Shirk: Worshipping or associating others with Allāh. Polytheism.

Ṣiddīqūn: Companions or close followers of the prophets. Literally, "one who confirms the truth."

Sijjīn: The lowest confines of Hell in which the record of evil deeds is inscribed.

Sūrah: A chapter of the Qur'ān.

Sulaymān: Solomon.

Sunnah: An established practice or tradition. All of the sayings, actions and silent approvals of Prophet Muḥammad (ﷺ).

Tābi'ūn: (Singular - *Tābi'ī*) Those who studied under the companions of the Prophet (ﷺ) Literally, "the followers."

Tafsīr: An explanation of the meanings of the Qur'ān.

Tawḥīd: Unification of Allāh. Monotheism.

Ummah: A community or nation.

Index of Ḥadīths[341]

Page

---

[341] This index does not include any of the weak , ḥadīths which appeared throughout the text.

Bibliography

Qur'ānic Sciences:

al-Ālūsī, Abul-Faḍl Maḥmūd, *Rūḥ al Ma'ānī fī Tafsīr al-Qur'ān al-'Aẓīm wa al-Sab' al-Mathānī,* pub. by Dār Iḥyā' al-Turāth al-'Arabī, Beirut, a republication of the Munīriyyah ed., *1933.*

'Abdul-Bāqī, Muḥammad Fu'ād, *al-Mu'jam al Mufahras li Alfāẓ al-Qur'ān,* Istanbul: al-Maktabah al-Islāmiyyah, *1984.*

al-Aṣfahānī, Rāghib, *Mu'jam Mufradāt Alfāth al-Qur'ān,* edited by Nadeem Marāshlī, Beirut: Dār al-Fikr, *1972.*

Bucaille, Maurice, *The Bible, the Qur'ān and Science,* USA: North American Trust Publications, *1979.*

Ibn Kathīr, al-Ḥāfiẓ Ismā'il, *Tafsīr al-Qur'ān al-'Aẓīm,* edited by Muḥammad Ibrāhīm al-Bannā, et. al., Cairo: Dār al-Sha'b, *1971.*

Ibn Kathīr, al-Ḥāfiẓ Ismā'il, *Tafsīr al-Qur'ān al-'Aẓīm,* critically edited by Muqbil bin Hādī al-Wādi'ī, Kuwait: Dār al-Arqam, *1985.*

Jawharī, Ṭanṭāwī, *al Jawāhir fī Tafsīr al-Qur'ān al-Karīm,* Cairo: Muṣṭafā al-Bābī al-Ḥalabī, *1930.*

Khān, Ṣiddīq Ḥasan, *Fatḥ al-Bayān fī Maqāṣid al-Qur'ān,* Cairo: Maṭba'ah al-'Āṣimah, *1965.*

al-Qur'ān al-Karīm, Cairo: Dār al-Muṣḥaf, *1971.*

al-Qurṭubī, Abū 'Abdullāh Muḥammad al-Anṣārī, *al-Jāmi'u li Aḥkām al-Qur'ān,* Cairo: Dār al-Qalam, *1966.*

al-Rāzī, Fakhrudīn, *al-Tafsīr, al-Kabīr,* Beirut: Dār Iḥyā' al-Turāth al-'Arabī, n.d.

al-Shanqīṭī, Muḥammad al-Amīn, *Aḍwā' al-Bayān fī Īḍāḥ al-Qur'ān bil-Qur'ān,* Cairo: Maṭba'ah al-Madanī, *1967.*

al-Ṭabarī, Abū Ja'far bin Jarīr, *Jāmi' al-Bayān 'an Ta'wīl Āyāt al-Qur'ān,* Egypt: Muṣṭafā al-Bābī al-Ḥalabī, *1968.*

al-Ṭabarī, Abū Ja'far bin Jarīr, *Tafsīr al-Ṭabarī,* edited by Aḥmad and Maḥmūd Shākir, Egypt: Dār al-Ma'ārif, n.d.

Ḥadīth Sciences:

'Abdul-Bāqī, Muḥammad Fu'ād, *Taysīr al-Manfa'ah,* Beirut: Dār al-Ḥadīth, *1984.*

'Abdul-Muṭṭalib, Rif'at Fawzī, *Ṣaḥīfat Humām bin Munabbih,* Cairo: Maktabah al-Khannjī, *1985.*

Abū Dāwūd, *'Awn al-Ma'būd Sharḥ Sunan Abī Dāwūd,* commentary by Abuṭ-Ṭīb Muḥammad Shamsul-Ḥaqq al-'Aẓīm-Ābādī, Madīnah: al-Maktabah al-Salafiyyah, *1968.*

al-Albānī, Muḥammad Nāṣiruddīn, *Ḍa'īf al-Jāmi' al-Ṣaghīr,* Beirut: al-Maktab al-Islāmī, *1982.*

al-Albānī, Muḥammad Nāṣiruddīn, *Manzilat al-Sunnah fil-Islām,* Kuwait: Dār al-Salafiyyah, *1984.*

al-Albānī, Muḥammad Nāṣiruddīn, *Ṣaḥīḥ al-Jāmi' al-Ṣaghīr,* Beirut: al-Maktab al-Islāmī, *1982.*

al-Albānī, Muḥammad Nāṣiruddīn, *Silsilat al-Aḥādīth al-Ḍa'īfah wa al-Mawḍū'ah,* Beirut: al-Maktab al-Islāmī, *1978.*

al-Albānī, Muḥammad Nāṣiruddīn, *Silsilat al-Aḥādīth al-Ṣaḥīḥah,* Beirut: al-Maktab al-Islāmī, *1958.*

al-'Asqalānī, Ibn Ḥajar, *Fatḥ al-Bāri bi Sharḥ Ṣaḥīḥ al-Bukhārī,* Cairo: al-Maktabah al-Salafiyyah, *1960.*

al-'Asqalānī, Ibn Ḥajar, *Tahdhīb al-Tahdhīb,* Beirut: Dār Ṣādir, reprint of Indian ed., *1905.*

'Aynī, Badruddīn, *'Umdah al-Qāri' Sharḥ Ṣaḥīḥ al-Bukhārī,* Cairo: Muṣṭafā al-Bābī al-Ḥalabī, *1972.*

al-Bayhaqī, Aḥmad bin 'Alī, *al-Sunan al-Kubrā*, critical editing by Ibn al-Turkmānī, Beirut: Dār al-Ma'rifah, reprint of Indian ed., *1924.*

al-Dārquṭnī, 'Alī bin 'Umar, *Sunan al-Dārquṭnī,* edited by Abuṭ-Ṭib Muḥammad Shamsul-Ḥaqq al-'Aẓīm-Ābādī, Madīnah: 'Abdullāh Hāshim al-Yamānī al-Madanī, *1966.*

al-Dārimī, 'Abdullāh bin 'Abdur-Raḥmān, *Sunan al-Dārimī,* edited by 'Abdullāh Hāshim al-Yamānī al-Madanī, Madīnah: *1966.*

al-Dhahabī, Muḥammad bin 'Uthmān, *Mīzān al-I'tidāl,* Cairo: Dār Iḥyā' al-Kutub al-'Arabiyyah, *1963.*

al-Dhahabī, Muḥammad bin 'Uthmān, *Siyar A'lām al-Nubalā',* Beirut: Mu'assasah al-Risālah, *1982.*

al-Fārisī, Alā'uddīn, *al-Iḥsān fī Taqrīb Ibn Ḥibbān,* an abridged version of Ibn Ḥibbān's *ḥadīth* collection, Madīnah: al-Maktabah al-Salafiyyah, *1970.*

al-Ḥākim, Abū 'Abdullāh, *al-Mustadrak 'alas- Ṣaḥīḥayn,* critically edited by al-Dhahabī, Beirut: Dār al-Kitāb al-'Arabī, n.d.

al-Haythamī, Nūruddīn, *Kashf, al-Astār ʿan Zawā'id al-Bazzār,* edited by Ḥabībur-Raḥmān al-ʿAẓamī, Beirut: Mu'assasah al-Risālah, *1979.*

Ibn al-Athīr al-Jazarī, Majduddīn bin Muḥammad, *al-Nihāyah fī Gharīb al-Ḥadīth,* Beirut: al-Maktabah al-Islāmiyyah, *1963.*

Ibn al-Athīr al-Jazarī, *Jāmiʿ al-Uṣūl fī Aḥādīth al-Rasūl,* critically edited by ʿAbdul-Qādir al-Arnā'ūṭ, Beirut: Maktabah Dār al-Bayān, 1969.

Ibn al-Ḥajjāj, Imām Muslim, *Ṣaḥīḥ Muslim,* Beirut: Dār Iḥyā' al-Turāth al-ʿArabī, n. d.

Ibn Ḥanbal, Aḥmad, *al-Musnad,* critically edited by Aḥmad Shākir, Cairo: Dār al-Maʿārif, 1954.

Ibn Ḥanbal, Aḥmad, *Musnad Aḥmad bin Ḥanbal,* Beirut: al-Maktab al-Islāmī, 1978.

Kandahlāwī, Muḥammad Zakariyyā, *Awjaz al-Masālik llā Muwaṭṭa', Mālik,* Beirut: Dār al-Fikr, 1980.

Mālik bin Anas, *al-Muwaṭṭa',* edited by Muḥammad Fu'ād ʿAbdul-Bāqī, Cairo: Dār Iḥyā' al-Kutub al-ʿArabiyyah, n.d.

Mubārakfūrī, Muḥammad ʿAbdur-Raḥmān, *Tuḥfah al-Aḥwāḍ,* Madīnah: al-Maktabah al-Salafiyyah, n.d.

al-Munāwī, Muḥammad ʿAbdur-Ra'ūf, *Fayḍ al-Qadīr,* Beirut: Dār al-Maʿrifah, 1972.

al-Nasā'ī, Aḥmad bin Shuʿayb bin Dīnar, *Sunan al-Nasā'ī,* edited and indexed by ʿAbdul-Fattāḥ Abū Ghuddah, Ḥalab: Maktab al-Maṭbūʿāt al-Islāmiyyah, 1986.

al-Qazwīnī, Ibn Mājah, *Sunan Ibn Mājah,* critically edited and computer-indexed by Muḥammad Muṣṭafā al-ʿAẓamī, Riyādh: Sharikah al-Ṭibāʿah al-ʿArabiyyah al-Suʿūdiyyah, 1983.

al-Qazwīnī, Ibn Mājah, *Sunan Ibn Mājah,* edited by Muḥammad Fu'ād ʿAbdul-Bāqī, Beirut: no publisher, n. d.

al-Ṭabarānī, Sulaymān bin Aḥmad, *al-Muʿjam al-Kabīr,* edited by Ḥamdī ʿAbdul-Majīd al-Salafī, Baghdād: Maṭbaʿah al-Ummah, 1980.

Tamīmī, Aḥmad bin al-Muthannā, *Musnad Abī Yaʿlā,* critically edited by Ḥusayn Salīm Asad, Damascus: Dār al-Ma'mūn lit-Turāth, 1984.

Wensinck, A. J. *al-Muʿjam al-Mufahras li Alfāẓ al-Ḥadīth,* Beirut: Reprint of 1943 Leiden ed., n.d.

ʿAqīdah:

al-Ālūsī, Nuʿmān bin Maḥmūd, *al-Āyāt al-Bayyināt fī ʿadam Samāʿ al-Amwāt,* critically edited by Muḥammad Nāṣiruddīn al-Albānī, Beirut: al-Maktab al-Islāmī, 1982.

al-Ālūsī, Nuʿmān bin Maḥmūd, *Jalā' al-ʿAynayn fī Muhākimat al-Aḥmadayn,* Makkah: Dār al-Bāz, n.d.

al-Ashqar, ʿUmar Sulaymān, *ʿĀlam al-Jinn wa al-Shayāṭīn,* Kuwait: Maktabah al-Falāḥ, 1983.

al-Ghazālī, Abū Ḥāmid, *Faḍā'iḥ al-Bāṭiniyyah,* Cairo: Dār al-Qawmiyyah, 1964.

al-Ghazālī, Abū Ḥāmid, *Maʿārij al-Quds fī Madārij Maʿārifat al-Nafs,* Dār al-Āfāq al-Jadīdah, 1981.

al-Ḥanafī, Ibn Abul-ʿIzz, *Sharḥ al-ʿAqīdat al-Ṭaḥāwiyyah,* critically edited by Muḥammad Nāṣiruddīn al-Albānī, Beirut: al-Maktab al-Islāmī, 1972.

Harrās, Muḥammad Khaleel, *Sharḥ al-Qaṣīdat al-Nūniyyah,* Cairo: Dār al-Fārūq al-Ḥadīthah, 1984.

Ibn Taymiyyah, Taqiyyuddīn Aḥmad, *Daru Taʿāruḍ al-ʿAql wa al-Naql,* edited by Muḥammad Rashād Sālim, Riyādh: The Islāmic University of Imām Muḥammad bin Suʿūd, 1979.

Ibn al-Qayyim, Shamsuddīn, *Hādī al-Arwāḥ ilā Bilād al-Afrāḥ,* Cairo: Maṭbaʿah al-Madanī, 1978.

Ibn al-Qayyim, Shamsuddīn, *Kitāb al-Rūḥ* critically edited by ʿAbdul-Fattāḥ Maḥmūd ʿUmar, ʿAmmān, Dār al-Fikr, 1985.

al-Jazāʾirī, Abū Bakr, *ʿAqīdat al-Muʾmin,* Cairo: Maktabah al-Kulliyyah al-Azhariyyah, 1977.

al-Khaṭīb, Muḥammad Aḥmad, *al-Ḥarakāt al-Bāṭiniyyah fil ʿĀlam al-Islāmī,* ʿAmmān: Maktabah al-Aqṣā, 1984.

al-Maydānī, ʿAbdur-Raḥmān Ḥasan, *al-ʿAqīdat al Islāmiyyah* wa *Uṣuṣuhā*, Damascus: Dār al-Qalam, 1979.

al-Nashshār, ʿAlī Sāmī, *Nashʾat al-Fikr al Falsafī fil Islām,* Cairo: Dār al-Maʿārif, 1977.

al-Qurṭubī, Abū ʿAbdullāh Muḥammad, *al-Tadhkirah fī Aḥwāl al Mawtā* wa *Umūr al-Ākhirah,* Madīnah: al-Maktabah al-Salafiyyah, n.d.

Safārīnī, Muḥammad bin Aḥmad, *Lawāmiʿ al-Anwār,* Beirut: al-Maktab al-Islāmī, 1985.

Salmān, ʿAbdul-ʿAzīz Āl-Muḥammad, *al-Kawāshif al-Jaliyyah ʿan Maʿānī al-Wāsiṭiyyah,* Riyādh: ʿAbdul-ʿAzīz Āl-Muḥammad Salmān, 1981.

Miscellaneous:

al-Albānī, Muḥammad Nāṣiruddīn, *Aḥkām al-Janā'iz wa Bid'uhā,* Beirut: al-Maktab al-Islāmī, 1969.

Ibn Kathīr, Abul-Fidā' Ismā'īl, *al-Bidāyah wa al-Nihāyah,* Beirut: Dār al-Kutub al-'Ilmiyyah, 1985.

Ibn Taymiyyah, *Majmū' al-Fatāwā,* collected and edited by 'Abdur-Raḥmān Muḥammad bin Qāsim, Rabāṭ: Maktabah al-Ma'ārif, n.d.

Ibn al-Athīr, 'Izzuddīn Muḥammad, *al-Kāmil fit-Tārīkh,* Beirut: Dār Bayrut and Dār Ṣādir, 1965.

The Bible, King James version, United Kingdom: the Gideons.